SIGN DESIGN

SIGN
SIGN
SIGN
SIGN
SIGN
SIGN
SIGN
SIGN
SIGN

SIGN DESIGN

Contemporary Graphic Identity

By the editors of
Signs of the Times magazine

PBC International, Inc., • New York

Distributors to the trade in the United States:

PBC International, Inc.
P.O. Box 678
Locust Valley, NY II560

Distributors to the trade in Canada:

General Publishing Co. Ltd.
30 Lesmill Road
Don Mills, Ontario, Canada M3B 2T6

Distributed in Continental Europe by:

Fleetbooks, S.A.
Feffer and Simons, B.V.
170 Rijnkade
Weesp, Netherlands

Distributed throughout the rest of the world by:

Fleetbooks, S.A.
c/o Feffer and Simons, Inc.
100 Park Avenue
New York, NY 10017

Library of Congress Cataloging-in-Publication Data

Main entry under title:

Sign design.

Includes index.

1. Signs and sign-boards.

I. Signs of the times (Cincinnati, Ohio)
HF5841.S525   1985   659.13'42   85-12134

ISBN 0-86636-013-1

Typesetting by Vera-Reyes, Inc.

Color separation, printing, and binding by
Toppan Printing Co. (H.K.) Ltd. Hong Kong

PRINTED IN HONG KONG
10 9 8 7 6 5 4 3 2 1

STAFF OF PBC INTERNATIONAL, INC.

Publisher:	Herb Taylor
Project Director:	Cora Taylor
Project Editor:	Linda Weinraub
Editor:	Carol Denby
Assistant Editor:	Carolyn Edwins
Art Director:	Richard Liu
Art Associates:	Charlene Sison
	Dan Larkin
	Daniel Kouw

STAFF OF SIGNS OF THE TIMES PUBLISHING COMPANY

Publisher:	Jerry Swormstedt
Project Director:	Bill Dorsey
Editor:	Tod Swormstedt
Art Consultant:	Magno Relojo

SIGN
SIGN
SIGN
SIGN
SIGN
SIGN
SIGN
SIGN
SIGN

Contents

FOREWORD   8

INTRODUCTION   9

1 Retail Stores   12

2 Restaurants and Hotels   66

3 Professional Services   108

4 Corporate Identification   130

5 Public Works   146

6 Real Estate   *166*

7 Experimental Work   *196*

8 Miscellaneous   *222*

INDEXES

    DESIGNERS   *248*

    FABRICATORS   *251*

    CLIENTS   *254*

DESIGN
DESIGN
DESIGN
DESIGN
DESIGN
DESIGN
DESIGN

Foreword

As evidenced by man's earliest cave drawings, signs have been a part of the social culture ever since there became a need to communicate. Whether one accepts or rejects this statement, it is well documented that signs, in the form of symbols, preceded the written word by eons, and that symbols remained the popular fashion of communication up until the late 19th century. It was only when the general populace became more literate that the use of the written word became widespread. That trend away from symbolism has continued today while only vestiges of the past remain.

As does any new design trend (and to be sure, the written word was exactly that) it took some time before it became realized. Many of the signs up until the mid 70s provided identification, but, too often at the exclusion of esthetic considerations. The signs of the 50s and 60s often met the identification need of the user, but in the total panorama, the streetscape was often cluttered with a jumble of commercial messages. This resulted in giving the industry a collective black eye continually poked at by zoning commissions, planning groups, and various organizations entrusted with the regulation of esthetics.

The philosophy behind the design of the on-premise identification sign has undergone more real change in the last ten years than it has in any period of its long history. It is no longer appropriate or acceptable for design to be weighed as a secondary ingredient to the sign message. A more sophisticated viewer with more discriminating taste requires the design quality's share equal consideration with a sign's identification criteria. Today, nothing less can be considered a successful design solution.

The design trend of the 80s appears to be going in two notable directions. One distinctive outlet is taking sign design to a clean look where identification to faster moving traffic is required; the other outlet is to an ornate, crafted appearance primarily intended to recapture the nostalgic seal of a time when the world moved slower.

The modern day sign industry is equipped and has access to the materials, lighting techniques, and engineering skills to meet these diverging needs. The product range includes steel, stainless steel, aluminum, a variety of plastics, woods, concrete, glass, gold leaf, paints and more, and a multiplicity of colors, textures, and patterns. From the illumination standpoint, the alternatives include direct, indirect, and silhouette lightings by fluorescent and incandescent lamps, floods, metal hallides, luminous tubing (neon) and even such light sources as lasers, and fiber optics.

Each material or combination of materials provides the necessary tools for the designer to construct solutions for the most challenging identity project. It is the object of this book to graphically illustrate a large number of significant sign identification solutions and, at the same time, showcase the functional design capabilities of the sign industry.

Jerry Swormstedt, Publisher, ST Publications

Introduction

Appreciation comes with understanding. To understand the eclectic nature of design in this book is to understand the nature of the sign industry itself. Just as the sign designs vary dramatically, so do the artists who conceive them and the craftsmen who fashion them. The conclusion to be made upon viewing this melting pot of talent is apparent: There really is no formal organization for sign per se in the entire industry. The work shown here is the product of a loosely organized, tenuously held together collection of the industry, which thrives and survives by its own tacit set of ground rules based on its own vision of the way things are. The end result in this book, simply but comprehensively titled: *Sign Design*.

The book is a celebration of possibilities, a reflection of creation without the constraint inevitably imposed by a single school of thought. *Sign Design* also demonstrates the skill and ability of an industry which is so apparent in everyday living that it continuously runs the risk of being ignored—or worse, being overlooked.

Wasn't this the statement being made by Andy Warhol in his now famous exhibit of Campbell soup cans? Wasn't Warhol really just showing the beauty of the commonplace? Wasn't he just trying to make us acknowledge the ''street art'' that is found all around us and continuously seeps into the collective unconscious?

In a somewhat different fashion, this book is attempting to do the same thing. This is nothing new. Reams of literature, in all sorts of industries, about all kinds of design endeavor to do the same. Some of this literature even focuses on the subject of this book. For instance, there are several magnificent tributes to the state of the neon art, such as Rudi Stern's *Let There Be Neon*. This admirably depicts one medium of sign design, as do similar volumes on airbrushing or outdoor advertising (billboards) or more specialized branches of sign design, such as *Corporate Design Systems 2* (published by PBC International).

Sign Design should be viewed in the total spectrum. Four hundred designs were selected from a pool of 10,000. They were often chosen for reasons other than being excellent examples of functional and attractive signs. In the compilation of *Sign Design*, the purpose was to represent as many designers, from as many industries, working in as many mediums as possible.

Among the craftsmen in the trade are the woodcarvers, the tubebenders, the gilders, the pinstripers, etc. These craftsmen represent what is commonly called the commercial sign industry. In terms of numbers, this is the largest part of the whole trade, representing perhaps, roughly speaking, 30,000 shops in the United States and Canada. There has never been an accurate census taken of this segment of the industry and there probably never will be. The reason for this stems from the way the industry is. It is comprised virtually of

DESIGN
DESIGN
DESIGN
DESIGN
DESIGN
DESIGN
DESIGN
DESIGN
DESIGN

SIGN
SIGN
SIGN
SIGN
SIGN
SIGN
SIGN
SIGN

thousands of one-person shops daily going about their business working off their homes. A listing in the phone book in the white pages, and not the yellow pages is quite frequently their only form of contact with the general public. Work either comes through subcontracting with the larger, established sign companies or by referral. Referral comes by establishing a reputation for quality and fairness.

In good times, the true craftsmen in the industry usually has more work than he or she can possibly handle. Despite the burdensome workload, the true craftsman rarely sacrifices quality for quantity. Long hours, isolation and little recognition is often the price the craftsman pays in exchange for a reasonably comfortable existence creating a product worthy of one's signature. The ultimate true craftsman's indelible stamp of approval appears on almost every page in this book.

In sharp contrast with the craftsman's fascination with a stylized form of embellishment, there exists another group of designers—a group which typically prefers its signs clean, uncluttered, highly legible, and always functional. This group has chosen to call themselves environmental graphic designers. Where the craftsman chooses Garamond or Playbill or some cursive form of typeface, the environmental graphic designer prefers to use typefaces like Helvetica or Helios or Optima. Where the craftsman designs a rustic, hand-carved Art Deco wood sign for a small restaurant in a resort community, the environmental graphic designer develops complex sign systems for office buildings, hotels, airports, zoos, universities, hospitals and various other forms of "architectural signing."

At the risk of stereotyping an industry that defies generalization, the environmental graphic designer usually works out of an office, and caters to upscale clients. Most have college educations and post graduate degrees in design, art, or architecture. Many of the designs appearing in "Corporate Identification" and "Public Works" are the product of this segment of the industry.

It's important to realize that, with few exceptions, environmental graphic designers rarely fashion what is drawn on the drafting table. The manufacturing end of things is usually left to their vendors—primarily the larger, custom electric sign companies. If the commercial sign industry can boast the largest numbers in terms of people, the custom electric industry can post the largest numbers in terms of sales volume. According to one census, this is a $2.3 billion market, divided up by an estimated 4,000 custom and quantity sign companies.

The custom electric sector represents the "Establishment" of the industry. It has a 40-year-old national association, which puts on four conventions per year. It has well-paid officers safeguarding its interests in Washington, D.C. It has a classically structured network of distributors who efficiently market the manufacturers' products down to the consumer.

Almost all custom electric firms employ at least one designer. Several of the largest companies (most notably in Canada) may number at least a half dozen art directors on staff. In the past decade, design (versus installation or maintenance) has become an essential service that determines the ultimate success or failure of a custom electric operation.

Indeed, in certain regional areas of North America, stiff competition among custom design companies has dramatically raised the level of graphic excellence in an entire area. To the discerning eye, the difference is noticeable. Major metropolitan areas that have received graphic facelifts, due primarily to the high quality of their custom sign firms, include Vancouver, British Columbia; Toronto, Ontario; Montreal, Providence of Quebec; Columbus, Ohio; and Seattle, Washington. And foremost among these areas is the industry's Emerald City, Las Vegas, Nevada.

The signs in these cities are constructed with a distinct and recognizable flair. Las Vegas, which has been described as the only "architecturally unified" city in the United States, is the most obvious example of a city in love with its signs. Yet, each of the aforementioned cities, even those with strict and restrictive sign codes, has developed its own look.

Design is as fickle as human perception is variable. Not much more than a decade ago neon stood as an undisputed symbol of garishness, the product of excess. Well, as a poet wrote, "The times they are a-changin'." Today, neon is all the rage.

The direction commercial design takes is based on too many unknown variables in the equation. The inherent danger in publishing any volume on design is in becoming outdated years before it becomes out of print. The risk is worth it in the knowledge that one satisfies a designer's inexorable and continuous quest for good design.

Bill Dorsey

SIGN SIGN
SIGN SIGN
SIGN SIGN
SIGN SIGN
SIGN SIGN
SIGN SIGN
SIGN SIGN

1

Retail Stores

Because of the variety of businesses involved, the chapter on Retail in this book shows the widest potential for design. While most of the other chapters are limited by a more specific type of business, this opening chapter is only limited by the *type* of business transaction, that is, retail vs. wholesale.

The result is apparent. Sign designs are as diversified as the businesses they identify. They can range from those highly readable monoliths which front an extensively traveled, high speed freeway to the very small, intricate signs which are aimed at pedestrian traffic.

Since the necessity for very large size somewhat restricts the design options available, this chapter (with some exceptions) concentrates on those signs directed toward the walking public. As the photos readily attest, this encompasses a plethora of materials and techniques.

DESIGN
DESIGN
DESIGN
DESIGN
DESIGN

Designer: James P. Ryan Associates, Architects
              and Planners
              Southfield, Michigan
Fabricator: Central Advertising
              Kalamazoo, Michigan
Client: Lakeview Mall

The pylon sign for Lakeview Mall is interiorly illuminated
with an acrylic face.

Designer: Normand Jalbert
Fabricator: Les Enseignes du Haut-Richelieu
               Quebec, Canada
Client: Le Pédalier

Sign consists of double 4 × 8-ft. faces.

Designer: Tom Graboski Associates, Inc.
               Coconut Grove, Florida
Fabricator: Graphic Systems, Inc.
               Coconut Grove, Florida
Client: Miami Lakes Athletic Club

Entire project is constructed of aluminum. Laminated
$3 \times 3 \times \frac{1}{8}$-in. thick squares are themselves laminated
with cut-out aluminum letters, figures and red stripe.
Major exterior ID is 5 × 5 ft. Two of the 8 × 8-in.
subsurface signs have been screen printed.

Designer: Normand Jalbert
Fabricator: Les Enseignes du Haut-Richelieu
Quebec, Canada
Client: Métamorphose Haute Coiffure

Sign consists of double 4 × 8-ft. faces mounted on a
corrugated metal base.

Designer: Neon Products Ltd.
                 Electroad Division
                 Vancouver, British Columbia, Canada
Fabricator: Neon Products Ltd. — Electroad
                 Division
Client: Cedar Wood Plaza

Sign is a 24-ft. high pylon using plastic neon and time
and temperature display; entire background of sign is
Cedar.

Designer: Paul White
Fabricator: Paul White Woodcarver
                 East Sandwich, Massachusetts
Client: The Potted Geranium

The sign has been completely carved out of wood, then
painted.

Designer: Curt Oxford Woodcarver
Fabricator: Curt Oxford Woodcarver
                Sebastian, Florida
Client: The Gazebo

The hand-carved Cedar sign has a flat green background with high-gloss coral lettering and trim

Designer: Mike Sheehan
Fabricator: Classic Sign and Mirror
                Pensacola, Florida
Client: Tallulah's Hair Design

The sign is sandblasted, double-sided Redwood with gold leaf letters and border, mounted on a single 4 × 4-in. pole.

Designer: Curt Oxford Woodcarver
Fabricator: Curt Oxford Woodcarver
Sebastian, Florida
Client: The Sun Spot

The sign is of routed and hand-carved clear Redwood.

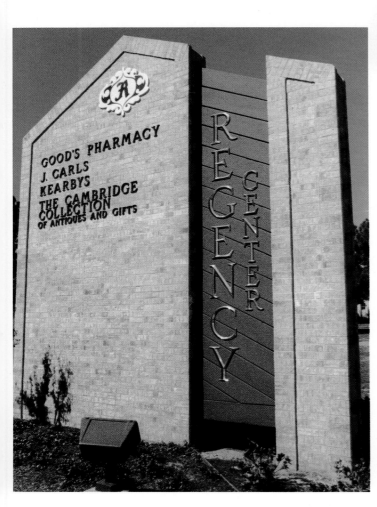

Designer: Jim Fancher
Barham Fancher Architects, Inc.
Tyler, Texas
Fabricator: Cavanaugh Art & Design
Flint, Texas
Client: Regency Center

The "Regency Center" sign features brass 16-in. and
9-in. letters against dark green enameled Redwood.
Names of individual shops in this exclusive shopping
complex are in dark brown acrylic 6-in. letters on the
cream brick entranceway. An ivory and brown crest, in
acrylic, continues the style.

Designer: W. Heath & Company
Fabricator: W. Heath & Company
Client: Wet 'n' Wild

Made in three sections, the sign is a set of fabricated
metal cabinets with plastic faces (small signs) and vinyl
face (large sign). All are internally illuminated with neon.
The wall letters are metal returns with plastic faces and
gold trim caps.

Designer: Media Concepts Corporation
Boston, Massachusetts
Fabricator: Paul McCarthy's Carving Place
Scituate, Massachusetts
Client: Schmid Music Box

The sign is hand-carved from $\frac{3}{4}$-in. Eastern Pine with the border and door canopy added.

Designer: Media Concepts Corporation
Boston, Massachusetts
Fabricator: Paul McCarthy's Carving Place
Scituate, Massachusetts
Client: Schmid Doll House

The $\frac{3}{4}$-in. Eastern Pine wood sign comes complete with attached, carved letters and top and bottom ornamentation.

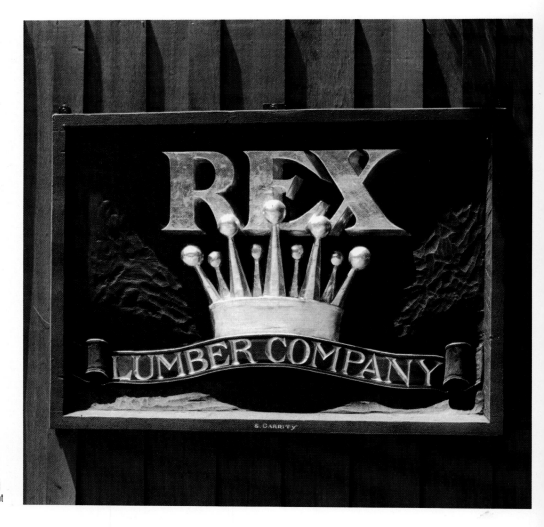

Designers: Susannah and Stephen Garrity
Fabricator: Garrity Carved Signs Company
    Belmont, Massachusetts
Client: Rex Lumber

Sign is hand-carved from 4-in. thick Mahogany, and measures 5 ft. 1 in. × 3 ft. 9 in. The crown spires were carved from a 6-in. thickness to achieve the desired three-dimensional effect. The background is dark textured brown with 23K gold. Three vertical steel brackets prevent bowing.

Designer: Ross Ireland
Fabricator: Cypress Carving Ltd.
    Vancouver, British Columbia, Canada
Client: Twigs

The sign is 32 in. high and is hand carved from solid Oak. The sign has been carefully enchanced with various colored antique glazes.

Designer: Michel Lajeunesse
Fabricator: Creation Vieil Art
    Granby, Quebec, Canada
Client: Le Vieil Art

The 16 × 25-in. Cedar has been routed, sandblasted, and sculptured. Lettering is gold leafed. The sign is designed with the company's trademark..

Designer: Mike Jackson
Fabricator: Jackson Signs
Moore, Oklahoma
Client: Claim Jumper Gift Shop

A suede leather oval has brass studs with rope around the perimeter, a head of weathered wood "made" from new Cedar, and 2-in. Redwood lettering that was sandblasted completely through.

Designer: James Pritchard
Fabricator: Pritchard Carved Signs
Peterborough, New Hampshire
Client: Mahfuz & Sons Rug Gallery

The sign is carved from laminated Eastern White Pine. The surface of the border was carved to resemble wood. The border design was done in lettering enamels and exterior gold paint. Copy is gilded.

Fabricator: Quality Signs & Designs
              Colorado Springs, Colorado
Client: Latigo

Clearheart Pine for an interior display was hand carved with routed edges, stained and clear lacquered. The flower was sandblasted.

Designer: Wendy Larrivee
              North Vancouver, British Columbia,
              Canada
Fabricator: Cypress Carving Ltd.
              North Vancouver, British Columbia,
              Canada
Client: Larrivee Guitars

The sign is hand carved from Western Maple and stained with alcohol-based guitar/violin stains. This is a copy of the label which appears inside the guitars. The guilded sign is used at tradeshows and for promotional displays.

Designer: Doug Simmons
Fabricator: Graphic Designs
Fayetteville, North Carolina
Client: Head to Toe

The sign is clearheart Redwood. The logo was routed, the copy sandblasted and trimmed with aluminum leaf.

Designer: Doug Simmons
Fabricator: Graphic Designs
Fayetteville, North Carolina
Client: The Mole Hole

The sign is of 2-in.-thick clear Redwood. Logo and copy have been shadowed with an airbrush.

Designer: Charles M. Crawford
Fabricator: Signs & Things
Naples, Florida
Client: Things from the Sea Scrimshaw

The 3-ft. diameter oval Cedar sign is double-sided and has been both sandblasted and carved. The sign is installed in a quaint waterfront shopping center called "Fin City" in Naples, Florida.

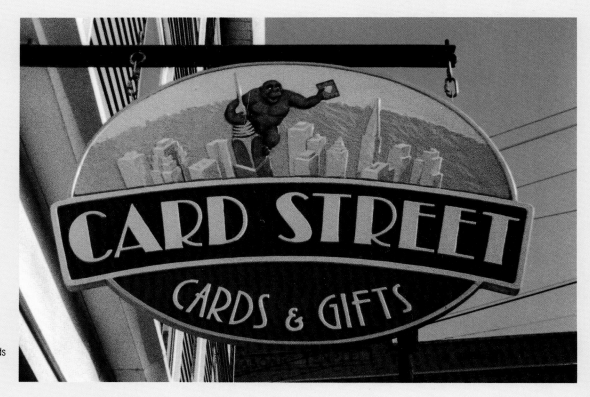

signer: Susan Bemel
Warwick, New York
ricator: Bemel Carved Sign
Pine Island, New York
ent: Card Street Cards & Gifts

e $\frac{5}{4}$-in.-thick Sugar Pine sign is double-faced. "Cards Gifts" letters are free hand routed. The pictorial is nted with silver highlights.

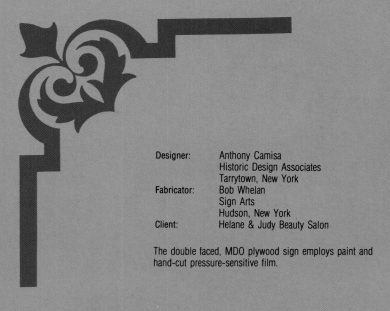

Designer: Anthony Camisa
               Historic Design Associates
               Tarrytown, New York
Fabricator: Bob Whelan
               Sign Arts
               Hudson, New York
Client: Helane & Judy Beauty Salon

The double faced, MDO plywood sign employs paint and hand-cut pressure-sensitive film.

Designer: Signs by Ben
Fabricator: Signs by Ben
               Bayfield, Wisconsin
Client: Maggie's

This hollow-bodied sign has a 2 × 4-in. frame covered with Cedar plywood. Sandblasted Cedar Panels, $1\frac{1}{2}$-in.-thick, are glued and screwed to the Cedar plywood. The outer frame and cove mold are of Redwood. The sign measures 36 × 54 in.

Designer: Jodie Adams Janssen
Fabricator: The Wood Shop
                Boyne City, Michigan
Client: Huff Pharmacy

The handcarved solid Mahogany sign is $3\frac{1}{2} \times 5$ ft. and employs 23K gilded letters. Bottles are sculpted and carved, then painted with acrylics.

Designer: Donald E. Woodsmith
Fabricator: Steamboat Woodsmith
                Steamboat Springs, Colorado
Client: Panache Sportswear

The double-sided Redwood sign, measuring 38 × 18 × 6 in., has a copper wrap and gold leaf lettering.

Designer: Gil Hayes
Fabricator: G.R. Hayes Signs
                  Broad Brook, Connecticut
Client: Violets & Victorian Lace

The sign is of 2-in. Redwood with a combination of hand-carved and routed letters and scroll. The blue background is recessed with simulated joints. Letters are gold leafed with dark blue outline.

Designer: Gary Anderson
Fabricator: Bloomington Signs
                  Bloomington, Indiana
Client: Bloomington Winery

The sign is flat painted on MDO plywood, then framed.

Designer: John Capon
               Capon & Austin Associates, Ltd
Fabricator: True Blue Design and Fabrication
               Markham, Ontario, Canada
Client: Market Lane

This 18 × 24-in. sign is of Sugar Pine,
edge-glued, sandblasted, and carved.

Designers: Jay Cooke, Greg Hyde
Fabricator: Jay Cooke's Sign Shop
               Stowe, Vermont
Client: Stowe Restoration

The main panel, of Honduras Mahogany, is hand carved,
with gold leaf used on the graphic and outside border.

Designers: Susannah and Stephen Garrity
Fabricator: Garrity Carved Sign Company
                 Belmont, Massachusetts
Client: Pharmacist

The 265-lb. "sign" is constructed with 14 plies of 12-in. thick Mahogany. Including the pestle, the overall dimensions are 39-in. high and 28-in. wide. Carving is gilded. The core is 30 percent hollow. The jar was shaped by hand.

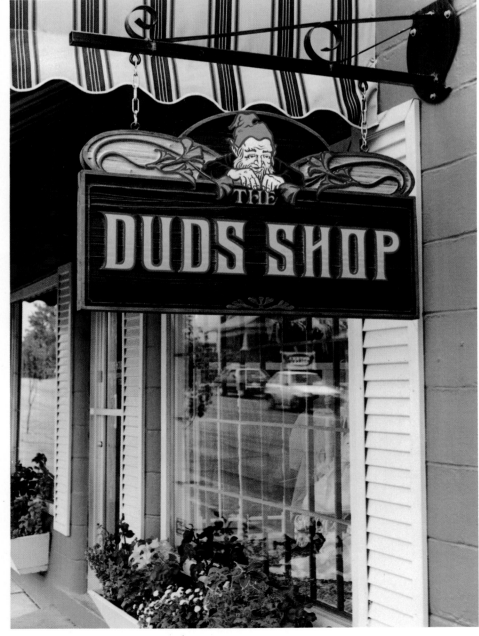

Fabricator: The Signmaker
                 Joplin, Missouri
Client: The Duds Shop

The sign was designed to complement the colors of the building and awning. It is double-faced, sandblasted Redwood, measuring 24 × 36 in.

Designer: Gary Anderson
Fabricator: Bloomington Sign
               Bloomington, Indiana
Client: Bellflower

Flat painted on plywood.

Designer: Ken Sorgman
Fabricator: Signs by Ken
               Santa Barbara, California
Client: The New York Bagel Factory

The 24-in. diameter Redwood bagel has been carved and airbrushed. The gilded letters are outlined in dark brown.

Designers: Douglas Williams, Media 5, and others
Fabricator: Douglas Williams, Woodcarving
              Haleiwa, Hawaii
Client: Victoria Ward Ltd.

All the signs in this shopping mall — 21 in all
representing shops, restaurants, restroom signs, and
directories — were carved from white Oak to match the
mall's white Oak paneling and trim. This provided a
unifying look while at the same time allowing individual
logos to provide separate identities.

Designer: Unica Design, Inc.
              Houston, Texas
Fabricator: The Mathis Company
              Houston, Texas
Client: Mr. Music

The painted wooden background has applied high-density foam letters.

Designer: Mike Longanecker
Fabricator: Hoarel Sign Company
              Amarillo, Texas
Client: Hub

Sign is 18-in. white 13mm skeleton neon, repeated five times. Neon is curved to fit the curve of the windows.

Designer: Chinook Plastics
Fabricator: Chinook Plastics
Calgary, Alberta, Canada
Client: Steele Jewellers, Ltd.

The facia sign butts up against a mirror which gives the appearance of a three-dimensional hanging sign. The fluorescent tubes shine through the semi-opaque mirror highlighting the $\frac{1}{2}$-in.-thick acrylic surface. The copy has been routed out.

Designer: James P. Ryan Associates, Architects
              and Planners
              Southfield, Michigan
Fabricator: Inner City Neon
              Counterline, Michigan
Client: Westland Center Shopping Mall
              Emporium

Sign is constructed of neon over mirror with painted
graphic.

Designer: Say It In Neon, Inc.
Fabricator: Say It In Neon, Inc.
              New York, New York
Client: Straight Lines

The exposed neon plays off stark decor.

Designer: Scott Riley
              Shillito/Rikes
Fabricator: City Lights Neon
              Cincinnati, Ohio
Client: Shillito/Rikes

The corporate logo identifies the junior's department. This
is just one sign which is part of a major renovation for
the entire department store. The sign employs coated
Noviol gold and white tubing.

Designer: Jeff Maple
              The Ramos Group
              Kansas City, Missouri
Fabricator: The Sign Shop
              Kansas City, Missouri
Client: Terrace Food Shops

The main section of the sign is constructed of .064
bronze with the copy routed out and backed with acrylic.
The other sections were fabricated from Oak with the
copy sandblasted and painted.

Designer: Daly & Daly
              Brookline, Massachusetts
Fabricator: Eller-United Outdoor Sign Company
              Fairfield, New Jersey
Client: Lucy's Marina Fun Center

The $4\frac{1}{2} \times 6\frac{1}{2}$-ft. carved wood sign was constructed for
a children's reception area at Harrah's Casino in Atlantic
City.

Designer: Henry Fells
Fabricator: Woodfox Designs
              Dalton, Pennsylvania
Client: Eadeh Rug Company

The sign is of 2-in.-thick Redwood, carved, stained, gold leafed, and outlined in red. Installed by LCA Sign Shoppe.

Designer: William J. Schnute
Fabricator: Oak Leaves Studio
               Iowa, City, Iowa
Client: The Hanger

The sign, measuring $2\frac{1}{2} \times 8$ ft., is carved from Redwood and colored with transparent house stains.

Designer: Henry Beer
               Communication Arts, Inc.
               Boulder, Colorado
Fabricator: Boulder Sign Studio
               Boulder, Colorado
Client: Risha

The sign is made of $\frac{1}{2}$-in. glass, backpainted and gilded. Outlines are 23K deep glass burnished gold; letter centers are water-gilded white gold varnished with airbrush gradation.

Designer: Sherry Snow
Fabricator: COMCO Architectural & Electrical
               Signing
               San Diego, California
Client: Harloff Chevrolet

The 2×8-ft. "H" structure is made of textured sheetmetal finished to match the building. The metal trim is finished in silver which matches the channel letters with the acrylic faces. "Harloff" has bronze acrylic faces backed with white acrylic for opposite effects in day and night.

Designer: Jim Dobney Art Service
             Las Vegas, Nevada
Fabricator: Heath & Company
             Las Vegas, Nevada
Client: Sound Emporium

The 12 × 32-ft. brushed aluminum "face" has white neon halo lighting around the edge of the display, behind the knobs, backlighted gauges and tape cartridge. The stereo store needed a strong identity because it is sandwiched between two other stereo stores.

Designer: The Sign Cellar
             North Conway, New Hampshire
Client: City Flair

The sign is made of $\frac{5}{8}$-in. MDO plywood and is framed and painted on both sides. The lettering was done by Chris Cormier.

Designer: James P. Ryan Associates, Architect and
               Planners
               Southfield, Michigan
Fabricator: Bob Glover, Inc.
               Clarkston, Michigan
Client: Ross Music

Clear acrylic letters, 1–in. thick, protrude through a gloss
black acrylic background with a painted pinstripe.

Designer: Christman Studios
Fabricator: Christman Studios
               St. Louis, Missouri
Client: West End Health Club

The window lettering employs enamel on glass.

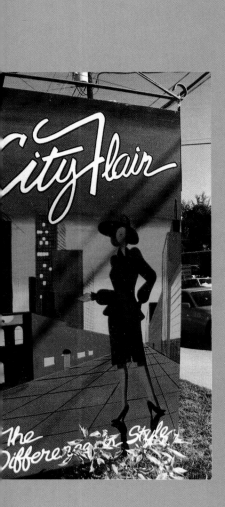

Designers: Andra Rudolph, Carl Rohrs
Fabricator: Carl Rohrs
                Santa Cruz, California
Client: Bodacious

The painted window identifies a plant store.

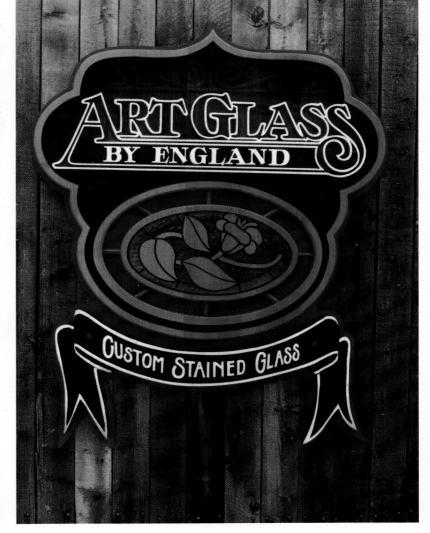

Designer: Mike Jackson
Fabricator: Jackson Signs
                Moore, Oklahoma
Client: Art Glass By England

The sandblasted Redwood has gilded and enamelled
lettering, a carved center oval and plywood backing and
border.

Designers: Stoltz Advertising, Satterfield Art
              Productions
              St. Charles, Missouri
Fabricator: Satterfield Art Productions
Client: Schnucks

The sign, measuring 24 × 36 in., was hand-carved from
8/4 Sugar Pine, and finished with polychrome enamel
and glaze.

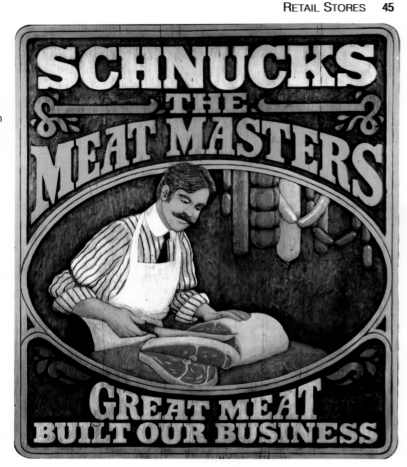

Designer: Gail Holiday
Fabricator: April Day Studio
             Columbia, Maryland
Client: Wilson's Harborplace Flower Market

The logo is screen printed on $\frac{1}{4}$ × 35 × 45-in. clear
acrylic for mounting on an interior window.

Designers: Mark Oatis, John Frazier
Fabricator: The Sign Studio
               Denver, Colorado
Client: 1421

For a fine antique store, the double-outline burnished numerals are in 23K gold and black. The center of the numerals are sunrises made out of abalone shell laid in varnish and outlined in 23K gold.

Designer: Charles Withuhn
Fabricator: Signs & Graphic Design
               Chico, California
Client: Chico Bicycle

The surface has been gilded on a separate piece of glass to achieve an extra texture and depth to the gold shadow. The outline is painted in. The bicycle on the top is variegated gold.

Designer: John F. Hannukaine Company
Fabricator: John F. Hannukaine Company
Tumwater, Washington
Client: Panowicz Jewelers

The main copy is outlined in both black and red and is
shaded with single-gild 23K matte centers. "Fifth &
Washington" lettering and flourishes are burnished 23K
goldleaf. Window is striped in 23K. The sign is
approximately 6 ft. wide.

Designer: Mark Oatis
Fabricator: The Sign Studio
Denver, Colorado
Client: Crown Glass Studio

A transom done in an art deco motif for an art glass
studio. The airbrushed effect was achieved by a blending
technique known as stippling.

Designer: Ancient Mariner
Fabricator: Ancient Mariner
               Vancouver, British Columbia, Canada
Client: Save on Foods

For a "Save on Foods" store, the interior signs employ a
system of backlit awnings.

Designer: Ancient Mariner
Fabricator: Ancient Mariner
              Vancouver, British Columbia, Canada
Client: Save on Foods

For a "Save on Foods" store, the interior signs employ a
system of backlit awnings.

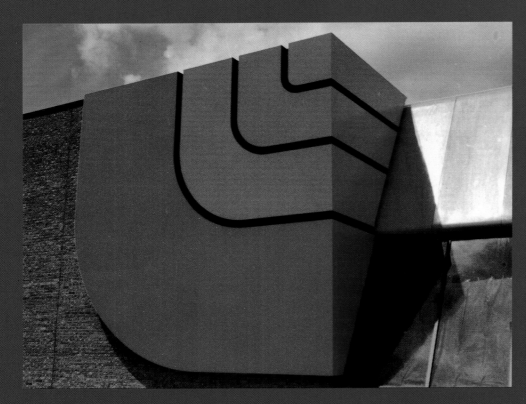

Designer: Don Watt + Associates
Fabricator: Acralume Signs + Displays, Ltd.
               Mississauga, Ontario, Canada

A non-illuminated aluminum logo, 22 × 22-ft. with a
13-in. return manufactured of $\frac{1}{8}$-in. aluminum with
baked enamel finish. The sign is manufactured in five
pieces and has no exterior screws or bolts.

Designer: Ralph Irwin
Fabricator: Art Forum, Inc.
Client: Home Builders Supply

The sign is primarily constructed over a plywood
structure and inset with stained glass. An existing plastic
sign was incorporated within the Victorian house. Every
piece was hand cut. Acrylic paints and primers were used
on the exterior. The sign is 26 ft. high, 12 ft. long, and 4
ft. thick. The clock functions and the weather vane works.

Designer: George Balsly
Fabricator: Dresden Graphics Sign Company
                Kansas City, Missouri
Client: Wardrobe Service

The design wraps around two sides of a four-story
building. Ultra Deep Base (custom mix) latex paint was
used.

Designer: Ken Smith
Fabricator: Ancient Mariner
Vancouver, British Columbia, Canada
Client: Contour Blind & Shade

Gloss vinyl ink has been sprayed on translucent PVC vinyl.

Designer: Roland Killian
             AIA Director of Design for the A.E.C.
             Group
             Springfield, Illinois
Fabricator: Arrow Sign Company
             A Division of White Way Sign Company
             Chicago, Illinois
Client: Egyptian Theatre

Molded terra cotta and a luminescent stained glass window make up the upper portion of this restored building's facade. The design relates to early Egyptian temple architecture, stressing frontal symmetry and strength.

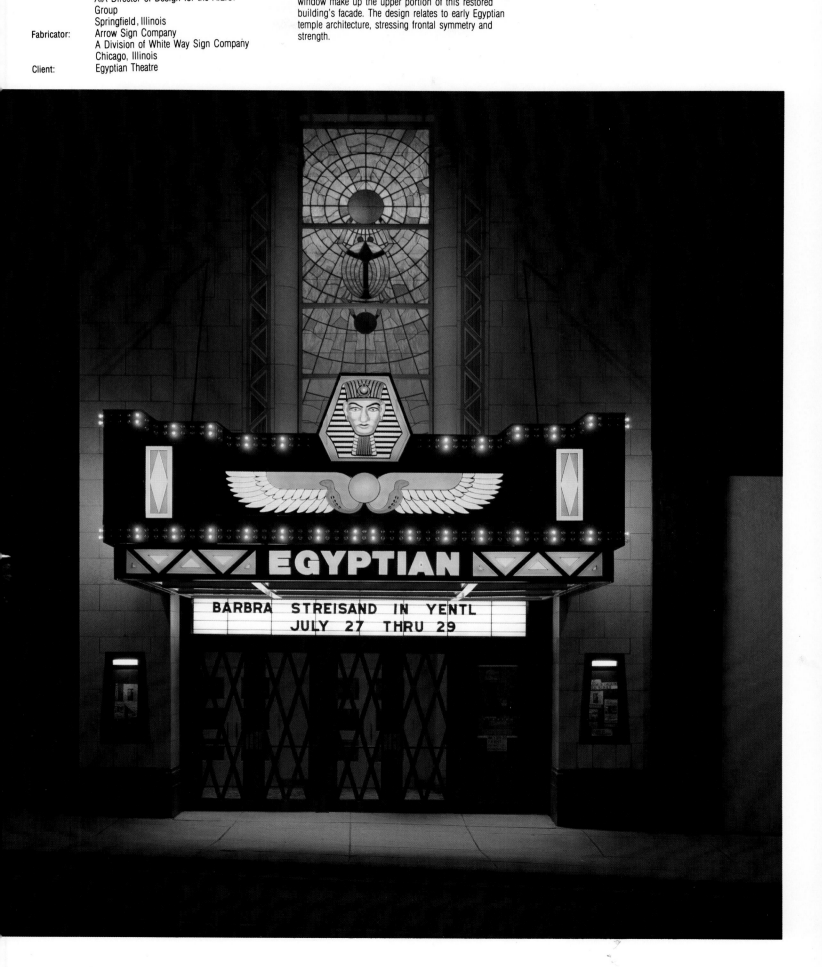

Designers: Ad Shoppe, Admiral Signworks
               Corporation
Fabricator: Admiral Signworks Corporation
               Virginia Beach, Virginia
Client: Very Virginia Beach

The sign is composed of .040 aluminum boxes with neon interiors, measuring approximately 60 ft. wide and 12 ft. high. The display is painted with automotive enamel. The word "Very" has channel letters in red neon on an 18-in.-deep background.

Designer: Ken Smith
Fabricator: Ancient Mariner
               Vancouver, British Columbia, Canada
Client: Futon to Sleep on

Gloss vinyl ink has been sprayed on translucent vinyl.

Fabricator: Ancient Mariner
              Seattle, Washington
Client: Temptations

The backlit awning was painted by Larry Wowk at Ancient Mariner's Seattle branch office.

Designer: Christman Studios
Fabricator: Christman Studios
             St. Louis, Missouri
Client: Martin Serenyo

The sign is backlit with maroon acrylic letters.

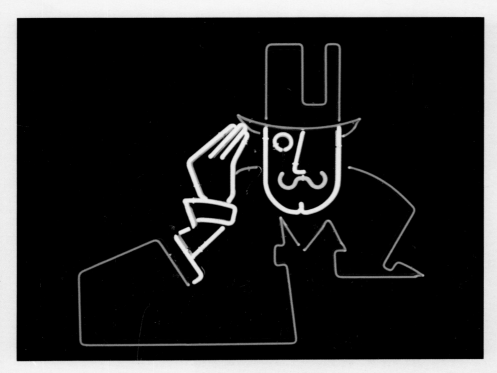

Designers: Jim Culbertson, Greater Pittsburgh Neon
Fabricator: Greater Pittsburgh Neon
                  Pittsburgh, Pennsylvania
Client: Jim Culbertson

The three-color neon wall graphic was commissioned for
a private home.

Designer: Bill Concannon, Sculptor
Fabricator: Aargon Neon
                  Benicia, California
Client: Fiorucci's

Concannon designed this piece for an upscale department
store.

Designer: Deco Neon
               Atlanta, Georgia
Fabricator: Deco Neon
Client: Scoops

The exposed neon sign for an ice cream parlor is 22 ft.
tall and employs neon chasers.

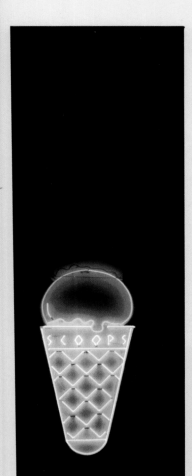

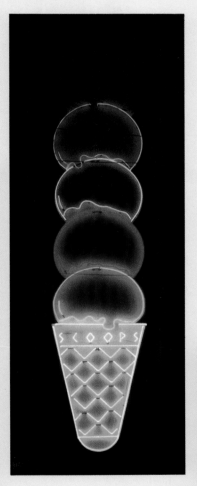

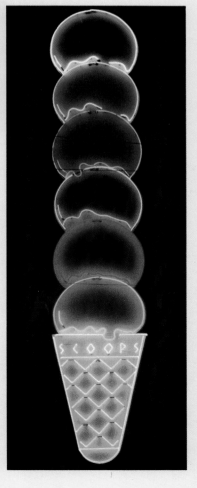

Designer: Deco Neon
               Atlanta, Georgia
Fabricator: Deco Neon
Client: Scoops

Designer: Storek + Storek
Fabricator: Neon Neon
              San Francisco, California
Client: My Child's Destiny

The neon lighting identifies the infant/toddlers department
of My Child's Destiny. Photo credit by Eve Humphreys.

Fabricator: Midtown Neon
              New York, New York
Client: Macy's

Neon display located in a Macy's department store.

Designer: Ted Bonar
Fabricator: Ted Bonar (now with Neon Projects)
              Washington, D.C.
Client: Aurora Borealis

The sign identifies a professional neon shop.

Designer: Mrs. Field's Cookies
Fabricator: Neon Neon
              San Francisco, California
Client: Mrs. Field's Cookies

Approximately 6 × 5 ft. in dimension, the sign is located in San Francisco and is one of two presently in existence. The second exposed neon sign, in Berkeley, California, was made smaller to conform to that community's more restrictive sign code.

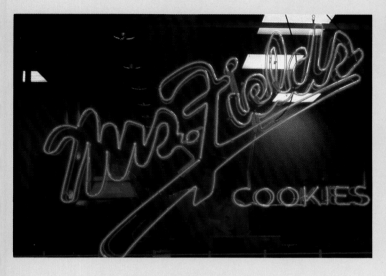

Fabricator: Neon Neon
              San Francisco, California
Client: Snoopy's Ice Cream & Cookies

The sign, photographed in San Francisco wharf area, identifies one of several Snoopy's ice cream parlors.

Designer: Arata Isozaki
Client: E.F. Hauserman

E.F. Hauserman's showroom, located in Chicago's Merchandise Mart, exemplifies the use of neon as an interior architectural highlight.

Designer: John Tanaka
Fabricator: John Tanaka
              New York, New York
Client: Lane Bryant

A neon point-of-purchase display for an upcoming sale.

Designer: Idea Design
Fabricator: Yerexneon, Inc.
               Scarborough, Ontario, Candada
Client: Faces

Neon sign is 60 in. tall by 42 in. wide.

Designer: G. Garnett
Fabricator: Sculptured Neon Company
               Fort Worth, Texas
Client: Dallux

A portable display sign advertising the Dallux tradeshow,
the ''DMC'' stylized logo stands for Dallas Marketing
Centers. The cabinet is black with a smoked-acrylic
display board.

Designer: Innervisions for Hair
               Newport Beach, California
Fabricator: Environmental Graphic Arts
               Huntington Beach, California
Client: Innervisions for Hair

This mural in the shampoo room is a handpainted latex
print measuring approximately 8 × 20 ft.

Designer: Allpoints Advertising
Fabricator: Allpoints Advertising
               Eureka, California
Client: Eureka Florist

The chrome look is employed for this florist shop. Note
the horizon line in the middle of each letter.

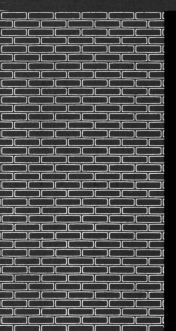

Designer: Michel Lajeunesse
Fabricator: Creation Vieil Art
               Granby, Quebec, Canada
Client: Shop 27

The 2-in. thick sign is cut very deep around the logo.
The sign identifies a disco situated in the entrance of an
old brick factory. Overall dimensions are 3 × 6 ft. Sign
was finished in enamels.

2

Restaurants and Hotels

It's always nice to provide quality to those who understand its value. Perhaps that is why so much care and thought is given to designing signs for restaurants, hotels and entertainment facilities. The owners of these establishments, in most cases, already comprehend the importance of good design. Their businesses are built on projecting a coordinated, coherent theme which captures the attention of the public. This extends to all aspects of their operations—including the design of their signs.

DESIGN
DESIGN
DESIGN
DESIGN
DESIGN

Designer:	Art Group, Inc.
	Pittsburgh, Pennsylvania
Fabricators:	Other Sign Company
	New York, New York
	D.C.A.
	Warrington, Pennsylvania
	Sziba & Smolover Glass Carvers
	New York, New York
	Friedman Marble & Slate
	Long Island, New York
Client:	Trumps

The entire system (only a part is shown here) employs a
variety of techniques and materials for the Atlantic City
Hotel Casino. The primary identification, Trumps, is 40
in. high and 18 in. deep and constructed of fabricated
brass letters standing on a marble base. This was
fabricated by Other Sign Company. Sziba & Smolover
Glass Carvers handcarved "Jezebel's" out of $\frac{3}{4}$-in. glass
framed in brass.

Designer: White Lettering & Art
Fabricator: White Lettering & Art
              Blountville, Tennessee
Client: Firehouse Bar-B-Que

The sign identifies an old firehouse which has been converted to a restaurant. The top faces are sandblasted in Western Cedar. The bottom faces are made from siding with Redwood letters sandblasted and then attached.

Designer: Artglo Sign Company
Fabricator: Artglo Sign Company
              Columbus, Ohio
Client: Tamarack Restaurant & Lounge

The architectural cubes create a modern sculptured effect which matches the contemporary tone of the building in which the restaurant is located.

Designer: Pat Culler
               Culler + Associates
               Dallas, Texas
Fabricator: Matthews International Corporation
               Architectural Sign Division
               Pittsburgh, Pennsylvania
Client: Anatole Hotel
               Dallas, Texas

Polished brass and a 4-in.-thick acrylic cube combine to create a look of elegance for a very exclusive French restaurant.

Designer: Ad-Art
Fabricator: Ad-Art
              Las Vegas, Nevada
Client: Oasis Casino

Each tree is constructed of $1\frac{1}{2}$ miles of neon tubing
backed by mirrored plastic. A computerized timing
mechanism sets in motion the lights which travel from
the bottom to the top of the palm trees' fronds.

Designer:	Young Electric Sign Company
Fabricator:	Young Electric Sign Company
	Las Vegas, Nevada
Client:	Paddlewheel

The sign is made of sheetmetal, polished aluminum gold, plastic, light bulbs, and exposed neon. The letters are channel lit and outlined in neon. The spokes are illuminated with neon, bulbs, and plastic balls. The wheel appears to turn by itself due to the combination of animated lights.

Designer: Cook's Sign Company
Fabricator: Cook's Sign Company
                 Cedar Falls, Iowa
Client: The Apartment Lounge & Grill

The 24 × 26-in. sign is constructed of MDO plywood, as well as Redwood and Oak.

Designer: Del McMillan Design Group Ltd.
                 Niagara-on-the-Lake, Ontario, Canada
Fabricator: Rustic Designs
                 Welland, Ontario, Canada
Client: George III

The 11 × 5-ft. Cedar sign features 3-in. thick cutouts.

Designer: Mike Keene
Fabricator: Signs by Mike
             Grand Lake, Colorado
Client: Club Car

The train car is cut out of Oak with smoked acrylic
windows and Oak veneer molding. The letters are made
of plywood with gilded faces and blue edges. The
background is plywood with a black felt covering.

Designer: Lesley Pritchard
Fabricator: The Wood Shop
             Boyne City, Michigan
Client: Inn the Woods

The oval sign is constructed of handcarved Pine with
gilded lettering.

Designer: Henry Fells
Fabricator: Woodfox Designs
              Dalton, Pennsylvania
Client: Hoffman House

The sign is constructed of 2-in. Mahogany. It is
double-sided and has been carved, stained, and gilded.
The edge is strapped with aluminum.

Designers: Susannah and Stephen Garrity
Fabricator: Garrity Carved Signs Company
              Belmont, Massachusetts
Client: Ferdinand's Restaurant

The double-faced sign is handcarved from Western Pine
and reinforced with wrought iron. The overall size is 40
× 45 in. Each side has its own "deep" bas-relief scene
painted in oil. The lettering is gilded in 23K gold.

Designer: Frank Barlow
Fabricator: Graphiconcepts
                 Garden City, Georgia
Client: River House Seafood

For a Georgia restaurant on Historic Riverstreet in
Savannah, Georgia, the sign is constructed of laminated
Redwood that has been sandblasted and carved. The copy
and fish are both gilded on this 4-sq.-ft. sign.

Designer: Donald E. Woodsmith
Fabricator: Steamboat Woodsmith
                 Steamboat Springs, Colorado
Client: The Cove

The double-faced carved Redwood sign is 32-in. in
diameter and has gilded letters.

Designer: Goldman & Associates
Oklahoma City, Oklahoma
Fabricator: Jackson Signs, Inc.
Moore, Oklahoma
Client: The Lodge

The double-sided identification has a carved background and moose head. letters are constructed of $\frac{3}{4}$-in. plywood.

Designer: Keg'n Cleaver
Fabricator: Ross Ireland, Cypress Carving Ltd.
Vancouver, British Columbia, Canada
Client:

Fabricated for one of more than 60 signs installed across Canada for the popular Keg'n Cleaver restaurant chain.

Designer: Doug Alcagi
             GNU Group
             Sausalito, California
Fabricator: Arrow Sign Company
             Oakland, California
Client: Ramada Inn

The double-faced, $4 \times 14\frac{1}{2}$-ft. monument sign is contructed with back-sprayed polycarbonate faces and fabricated brass letters.

Designer: Frank Mando
Fabricator: Graphic Solutions
              San Diego, California
Client: The Philadelphia Sandwich Company

The $2\frac{1}{2}$-in. thick Western Red Cedar sign was stained and hand rubbed to expose the grain, then hand lettered and rendered with a chipboard applique.

Designer: Gannett Outdoor of New Jersey, United
              Sign Division
Fabricator: Gannett Outdoor of New Jersey, United
              Sign Division
              Fairfield, New Jersey
Client: Pastabilities

The channel letters with the silver trim and smaller acrylic letters are pushed through stencil-cut openings and are internally illuminated. The white aluminum frame has polished returns and molding.

Designer: James Galloway
Fabricator: Galloway Signs
               Cincinnati, Ohio
Client: Izzy's

A carved foam sculpture employs reflective film. "Famous corn beef" is routed out while the frame is laminated to the foam, painted with acrylic colors, and finished in polyurethane.

Designers: Jay Cooke, Rick Loya
Fabricator: Jay Cooke's Sign Shop
              Stowe, Vermont
Client: McDonald's

The $6\frac{1}{2}$-sq.-ft. sign was designed for a city which does not permit plastic or internally illuminated signs. The logo has been sandblasted. Letters are hand carved.

Designers: William and Ronda Schnute
Fabricator: Oak Leaves Studio
              Iowa City, Iowa
Client: McDonald's

Ronald McDonald was hand carved by William and Ronda Schnute from a lightning-struck Douglas Fir tree. A handcarved squirrel (not pictured) climbs up the side of the 12-ft. high stump.

Designer: Raymond Gariepy
Fabricator: Enseignes Poitras, Inc.
Quebec City, Quebec, Canada
Client: Maison Milot

The double-sided sign is made of wrought iron and painted wood and conforms to the old style of architecture which exists in historic Quebec City.

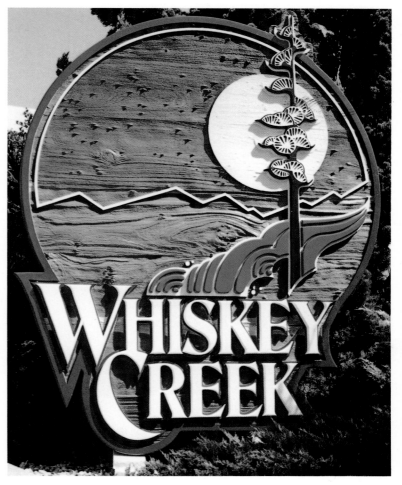

Designer: Sarah Fine
Mammoth, California
Fabricator: Sawdust Creations
Costa Mesa, California
Client: Whiskey Creek

A sandblasted, kiln-dried Redwood wall sign has applique letters and designs. This is constructed for a fine foods restaurant in Mammoth, California, a summer mountain and ski resort.

Designers: Raymond Gariepy, Maurice Poitras
Fabricator: Enseignes Poitras, Inc.
Quebec City, Quebec, Canada
Client: Vérité Mensonge

The 5 × 8-ft. painted wood sign has gilded lettering.

Designer: Kirk Van Swearingen
Fabricator: Ten Mile River Sign Company
                Wingdale, New York
Client: Buffalo Gals Restaurant

The pictorial has been painted on this hanging wood sign.

Designer: Richard Runquist
Fabricator: First Impression Sign Company
                Chico, California
Client: Canal Street

The airbrushed letters complement the 5 × 10-ft. painted sign.

Designer:	Simco Sign
	Everett, Washington
Fabricator:	John F. Hannukaine Company
	Tumwater, Washington

"Billy's" is lettered with single-gild matte centers with a black outline and maroon double outline. "Bar & Grill" is lettered with single-gild matte centers with a black outline on a solid maroon panel. The gray window border is screen printed and hand striped.

Client: Navarre Cafe

The sign was gilded circa 1920 and employs a burnished outline in 23K gold. Centers are 18K and 16K variegated gold with crossed leaves and a triple-split green shade. It is approximately 3 ft. long and 6 in. high.

Designer:	H. Langhorst
	On Board Signs
Fabricator:	On Board Signs
	Dunedin, Florida
Client:	Smuggler's Cove Cafe

Cedar siding has been used as a background to mirror the siding on the building. The sign is Cedar and hand carved with gold leaf copy.

Designer:	Kirk Van Swearingen
Fabricator:	Ten Mile River Sign Company
	Wingdale, New York
Client:	Squire's East

One of three window signs for a Poughkeepsie, New York, bar and grill, the lettering is 30 in. wide.

Designer: Neal Fuller
Fabricator: Nu Art Signmaker
Santa Ana, California
Client: Avanti Trattoria

Dark blue ceramic tile was mounted in a wood frame and hung from a wrought iron structure. The gilded copy was then sandblasted and outlined in peach. The same peach color was used for the bottom copy.

Designer: Tarnoff Graphics
Los Angeles, California
Fabricator: Southcoast Designs
Corpus Christi, Texas
Client: The Lighthouse

The sign measures 8 × 7 ft. and is made of laminated clearheart Redwood. Copy for "The Lighthouse" is in four levels of relief, sandblasted and routed; the letter shadows are airbrushed. Copy for "Fresh Seafood & Libations" has a sandblasted background. The rock area, as well as the sky, oceans, boats, and skyline are hand carved. The sky and water are airbrushed; the borders are gold leafed.

Designer: Gardner Signs, Inc.
Fabricator: Gardner Signs, Inc.
             Fort Collins, Colorado
Client: Laurel Street Station

The open-faced pan channel display has exposed neon tubing installed on face of the canopy.

Designer: Robin A. Bohlman
Fabricator: Dwinnell's Central Neon Company
             Yakima, Washington
Client: Lake Cafe

The exposed neon is constructed on a double-faced sheetmetal sign with accent lines. "Union" center is made of acrylic with internal illumination. The ends of the cabinet are wrapped with an aluminum chrome finish as is the trim on the cabinet face. Overall dimensions are 6 × 11 ft.

Designer: Signs Systems, Inc.
Fabricator: Sign Systems, Inc.
             Las Vegas, Nevada
Client: Hilton

The backlit awning incorporates the superstructure's framework into the design.

Designer: Inner City Neon
               Centerline, Michigan
Fabricator: James P. Ryan Associates, Architects &
               Planners
               Southfield, Michigan
Client: Picnic

The sign identifies "Picnic Food Court" in the Lakewood Mall, Battle Creek, Michigan. It uses neon on a glass panel.

Designers: David Jenks, Sharon Griffin of the
                Design Group
Fabricator: University of Washington Sign Shop
                Seattle, Washington
Client: Portage Bay Galley

Each area of the "servery" offers a different set of menu
items and is distinguished from the other areas by the
coordinated colors of the canvas signs and the menu
boards. The stretched canvas signs suspended from the
ceiling use brass grommets, polyester braid, and PVC
pipe frame.

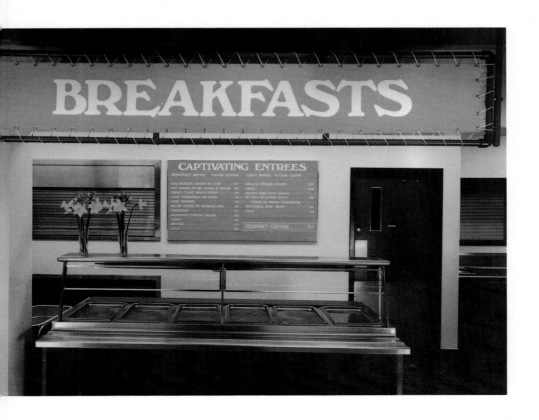

Designer: United Signs, Inc.
Fabricator: United Signs, Inc.
              Cincinnati, Ohio

The sign is constructed of fabricated sheetmetal. The open channel letters are exposed and outlined in neon. The raceway below the sign's letters has running lights.

Designer: Robert Markle
Fabricator: Yerexneon, Inc.
              Scarborough, Ontario, Canada
Client: Markleangelo's Restaurant

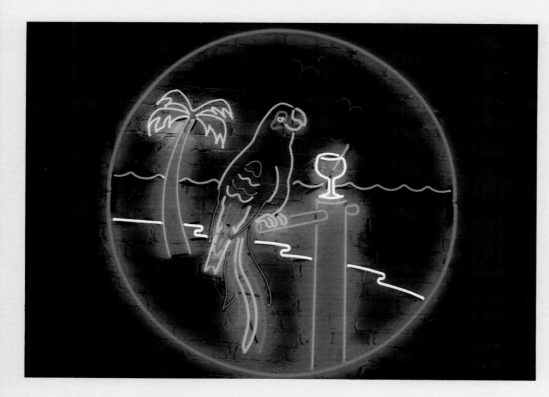

Designer: Dr. Neon
Fabricator: Dr. Neon
               Austin, Texas
Client: Green Parrot Restaurant & Bar

An interior piece for a restaurant/bar located in San Marcos, Texas, the parrot displays various shades of neon: bromo, ruby, apple, jack green, and noviol gold. The unit is mounted with silicone to stand-offs attached to the brick wall for a very clean look without tie wires. Diameter of the circle is 60 in.

The 4 × 6-ft. sign was originally discovered without the glass and with a face that read "Central Billiards." Michael Yerex restored the art deco stainless steel and glass enamel face to its original condition and added the restaurant's logo.

Designer: Karen Heisler
Fabricator: Neon Neon
San Francisco, California
Client: Expresso Yourself

The neon sign is for a coffee house.

Designer: Bill Concannon
Fabricator: Bill Concannon, Sculptor
Venice, California
Client: Paradise Cafe

The sign is approximately 3 × 8 ft. in dimension and was created for a Long Beach, California cafe.

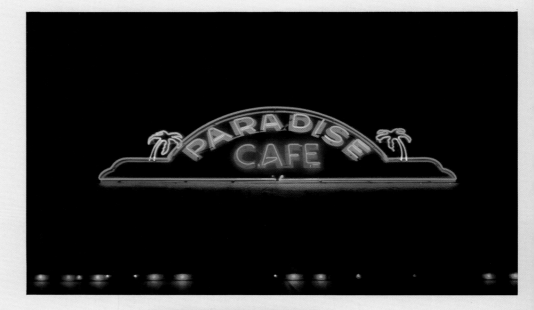

Designer: Sam DuVall (Ritz Cafe owner)
Fabricator: Local Neon Company, Inc.
Santa Monica, California
Client: Ritz Cafe

The 23 × 7-ft. sheetmetal sign is constructed in three layers of green and gold neon. "Ritz" is 12 in. deep; the "Cafe" is 3 in. back; the chevrons are 3 in. behind "Cafe."

Designer: Mike Stevens
Fabricator: Hollinger, Stevens
Akron, Pennsylvania
Client: Golden Gate Theatre

The 18 × 26-in. showcard was lettered
extemporaneously.

Fabricator: Neon Neon
San Francisco, California

The exposed neon sign identifies Bette's Ocean View
Diner. Photo credit by Eve Humphreys.

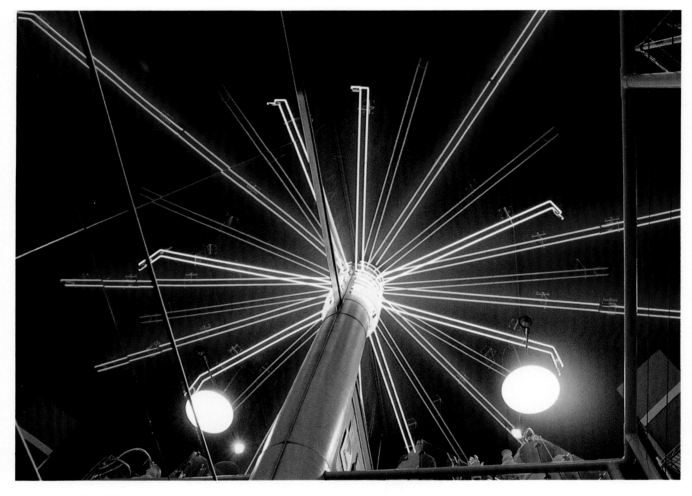

Designer: Fiory & Wong
Fabricator: Neon Neon
               San Francisco, California
Client: Headlines

The exposed neon identifies San Francisco's night spot.

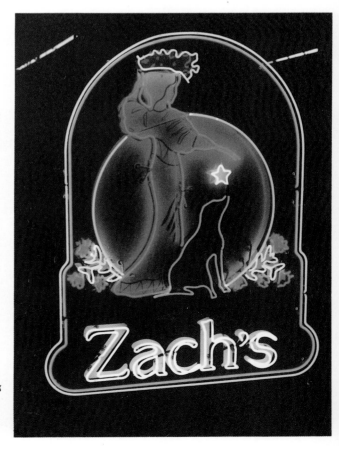

Designer: Jim Collender
Fabricator: Lite Craft Neon, Inc.
               Boulder, Colorado
Client: Zach's

The sign employs exposed 8-15 mm neon set in a black cabinet. The owner, whose dog was named after the restaurant, reportedly liked the sign so much he later ordered a rose and green frame of border tubing for the restaurant's facade.

Designer: Dr. Neon
Fabricator: Dr. Neon
             Austin, Texas
Client: Platters Cafe 1955

The Cadillac is mounted on 5 × 10-ft. modified acrylic. The record is controlled by three-channel programmable electronics. The flamingo has ruby-red glass knee joints.

Designer: Robert Costa
Fabricator: Greater Pittsburgh Neon
                Pittsburgh, Pennsylvania
Client: Peerless Wallpaper

Entitled "Peerless Theatre," the seven-color piece is
10 × 30 ft. in dimension.

Designer: Creative Design
                Seattle, Washington
Fabricator: Light Images, Inc.
                Spokane, Washington
Client: Ankey's

The 12mm glass sign is mounted on $\frac{1}{3}$-in. mirror set 5
in. behind black tinted glass.

Designer: Tony Sikorski Studio
Pittsburgh, Pennsylvania
Fabricator: J&K Sign Company
Aliquippa, Pennsylvania
Client: The New York Deli

The 2 × 18-ft. plastic face sign uses clear letters with a painted shadow. The sign is illuminated with a neon New York skyline.

Photo courtesy of the Retail Reporting Bureau, New York, New York.

Designer: Graphic Systems
Fabricator: Signtific Signs
              Tucson, Arizona
Client: Sheraton Tucson El Conquistador

A screen print on Flexiglas is the second surface for Desert Spring.

Designers: Douglas Williams, Gib Black &
              Associates
Fabricator: Douglas Williams, Woodcarving
              Haleiwa, Hawaii
Client: Captain's Table

The restaurant is done in early passenger-shop motif. The sign is carved from Redwood, with "Captain's Table" lettering in gold leaf with black outline.

Designer: Sign Wizards
Fabricator: Sign Wizards
               Marshfield, Wisconsin
Client: Kathy's Pub

The sign is constructed of Redwood painted with
one-shot. The inside of the sign is connected to the
outside rim by 35 gallery spindles. The rim is
sandblasted, while the inside circle is carved.

Designer: Ross Ireland
Fabricator: Cypress Carving Ltd.
               North Vancouver, British Columbia, Canada
Client: Mother Hyde's Kitchen

The signboard and letters are of solid Oak. The letters
were hand carved and applied to the face; the house was
carved from Jelutong, and stained, painted, and antiqued.
This is an interior sign.

Designer:	Neon Products Ltd.
Fabricator:	Neon Products Ltd.
	Vancouver, British Columbia, Canada
Client:	Hy's Encore

The sheetmetal canopy has exposed red neon lettering which highlights the client's shield. Overall dimensions are 11 ft. high and 7 ft. wide. The sign projects 5. ft.

Designer:	Neon Products Ltd. (logo provided by client)
Fabricator:	Neon Products Ltd.
	Willowdale, Ontario, Canada
Client:	Brandy's

The 7-ft. wide by 4-ft. high sign is internally illuminated and constructed on a backlit canopy.

Designer: Ross Ireland
Fabricator: Cypress Carving Ltd.
                 Vancouver, British Columbia, Canada
Client: The Keg Lobster House

The cut-out wood letters butt up against a brick wall.

Designer: Graphic Designs
Fabricator: Graphic Designs
                 Fayetteville, North Carolina
Client: Sweet Caroline's

"Sweet Caroline's" primary sign is constructed of sandblasted clearheart Redwood that has been reinforced to the wall with a metal frame. The information signs (below) are handpainted on $\frac{1}{2}$-in. plywood.

Designer: Graphic Systems
Fabricator: Signtific Signs
Tucson, Arizona
Client: Sheraton Tucson El Conquistador

A brass and copper logo wall mount for Sundance.

Type is mounted on a fabric background with a brass border. The logo for Victoria's is sandblasted on the glass door of the restaurant.

Designer: Donald E. Woodsmith
Fabricator: Steamboat Woodsmith
Steamboat Springs, Colorado
Client: Cantina

The sign, measuring 11 × 3 ft., is of carved Redwood. The three-dimensional face has a gold-leafed tooth; the painting is hand brushed.

Fabricator: Artistic Signs
               Slidell, Louisiana
Client: Lil' Ray's Po Boys

The sign is of 2-in.-thick Redwood, laminated
and cut to shape, then sandblasted and painted.

Designer: Roger K. Smathers
Fabricator: Signs South
               Greenville, South Carolina
Client: M.R. Ducks

The 6 × 8-ft. sign is of sandblasted clearheart Redwood.

Designer: Glenn Monigle & Associates, Inc.
Denver, Colorado
Fabricators: Ellis Doughty, Jerry Swanson, Paul Corbin
Western Sign Company
Tulsa, Oklahoma
Client: Theatre mural

The 60-ft. long graphic was painted on a vinyl-covered wall using bulletin enamels and charcoal.

Designer: Ron Rodgers
Fabricator: Rodgers & Wiley
               Fremont, California
Client: Niles Hotel and Bar

The 7 × 10-ft. mural was painted on plywood with bulletin enamels. It depicts the 1908 Niles concert band posing in front of the old Niles train station. The station has been remodeled as a Victorian-style hotel and bar offering live entertainment.

Designer: Francis Pedley
Fabricator: Francis Pedley
               Moosomin, Saskatchewan, Canada
Client: Last Spike

The 8 × 12-ft. mural entitled the "Last Spike" is one of three which were designed and painted for a bar/restaurant in Regina, Saskatchewan.

3

Professional
Services

Those who offer professional services to the general public are in a curious position: They want and need the business; but they don't want to be obvious about it. The theory being—if you are good people will know it. For whatever reason, it's usually considered highly unprofessional for the professional to advertise for customers. A doctor who too brashly boasts his abilities runs the risk of appearing the charlatan; as does the lawyer, and the accountant. For these reasons, most professionals opt for understated, elegant identification.

Bankers use to follow the same guidelines but now, the banking industry, deregulated and now highly competitive is an exception to the rule of understatement. Strength and stability must be communicated but the bank's identity and message must be presented loud and clear. The advertising posture of the banking community is one of a very high profile. This is, in part, reflected by its signs—bold, graphic, and in many instances, complete with attention grabbing time and temperature readouts.

What follows here are signs that show understatement where required and boldness where needed.

DESIGN
DESIGN
DESIGN
DESIGN
DESIGN
DESIGN

Designer: Keith Knecht
Fabricator: Signs & Things
               Naples, Florida
Client: Signs & Things

For its own signage, the company chose sandblasted
Redwood, with a black glass smultz background and
copper letters with a glo-blue outline.

Designer: Andresen Typographics
Fabricator: Fine Gold Lettering
                Harbor City, California
Client: Andresen Typographics

The 20-in. "A" combines 23, 18, 16 and 12K gold with
a silver burnish, and japan and abalone accents.

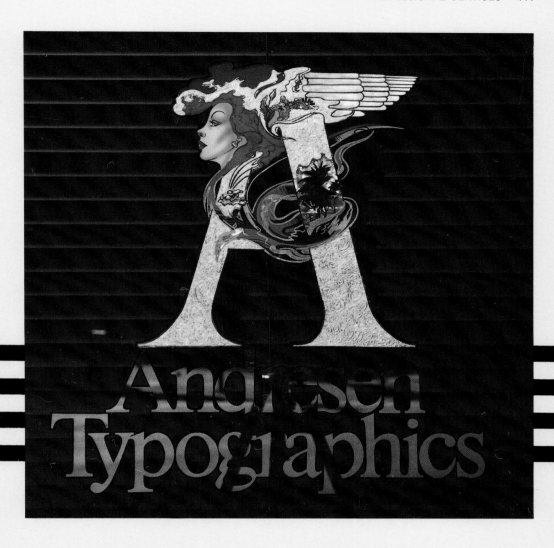

Designer: Gary Anderson
Fabricator: Bloomington Sign
                Bloomington, Indiana
Client: Academy of Russia Classical Ballet

The sign is flat-painted on MDO plywood.

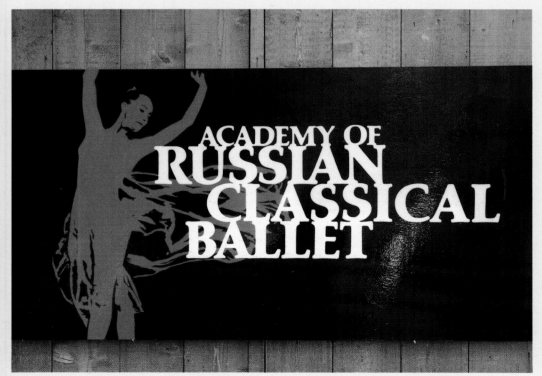

Designer: Jim Carter
Fabricator: Olson Signs & Displays
                   Scotia, New York
Client: The Creative Advantage, Inc.

The client's logo and the border are raised and routed out of two pieces of $2\frac{3}{4}$-in. duraply, and painted. Other printed material is silkscreened.

Designer: Mike Jackson
                  Moore, Oklahoma
Fabricators: Jackson Signs and Michel Lajeunesse,
                  Creation Vieil Art
                  Granby, Quebec, Canada
Client: Jackson Signs

The self-promotional "hand" was hand carved by Michel Lajeunesse.

Designer: Clement Micarelli
Fabricator: Paul McCarthy's Carving Place
                   Scituate, Massachusetts
Client: Micarelli/Warner Art Studio

The entire surface of the sign has been hand carved from 2-in.-thick Mahogany. All areas are softly rounded into each other.

Designer: David E. Jacome
Fabricator: Jacome & Company
Tucson, Arizona
Client: Jacome & Company

Designed for use in Tucson's historical business area, the sign displays the company's logo and type of business. Pieces of Redwood, each measuring 2 in., were glued together, primed, painted, and routed. Serifs were hand cut with an X-acto knife.

Designer: Dusty Yaxley
Fabricator: Letter Art Unique Signs + Advertising
New Port Richey, Florida
Client: Bob Overby Neonist

The 12 × 10-in. desktop sign is constructed of Mahogany with incised carved and gilded letters. The brass and steel wires are intended to imitate the effect of neon.

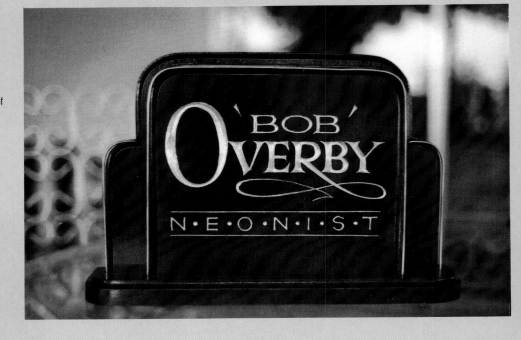

Designer: Ed Hannaman
Fabricator: Ed Hannaman Sign Crafters
Newville, Pennsylvania
Client: Ed Hannaman Sign Crafters

The lettering has been sandblasted into this 24 × 32-in. flashed glass sign.

Designer: Colorado Woodsmiths
Fabricator: Colorado Woodsmiths
Client: Colorado Woodsmiths

This is a handcarved Redwood sign with brass laminate
lettering and duraply cut letters backlit with high-output
fluorescent lights.

Designer: Ken Sorgman
Fabricator: Signs by Ken
Client: Signs by Ken

The sign features gold-leaf routed edging and
sandblasted stained glass panels

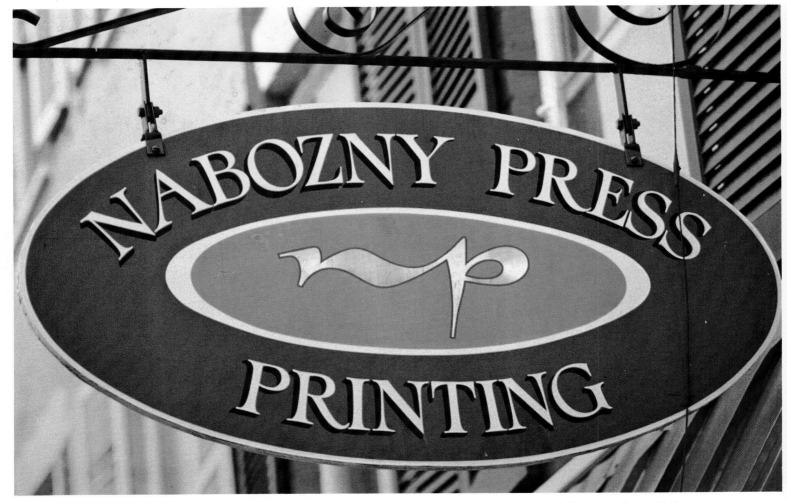

Designer: Raymond A. Ruge
Historic Design Association
Terrytown, New York
Fabricator: Bob Whalen
Sign Arts
Hudson, New York
Client: Nabozny Press

The double-faced elliptical sign has a gilded logo and custom bracket.

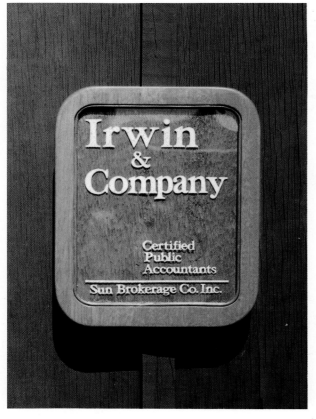

Designer: Henry Fells
Woodfox Designs
Dalton, Pennsylvania
Client: Irwin & Company

Framed with 2-in. Mahogany, the letters, lacquer with furniture finish, were placed on the backside of an acrylic rectangle.

Designer: John F. Hannuakaine
Fabricator: John F. Hannuakaine Company
Tumwater, Washington
Client: Broadway Dental Center

The 6 ft. high ground sign is constructed of Fir, Cedar, and Redwood with a stained finish. The letters are made of polyester with a 23K gilded finish.

Designer: Reg Namour
Fabricator: The Architecture Group
Charlotte, North Carolina
Client: Southwood Corporation

The 4-ft. diameter logo was routed into an exterior wall and painted with enamel colors.

Designer: Signs by Liza
Fabricator: Signs by Liza
               Naperville, Illinois
Client: Signs by Liza

The sign is painted in enamel and 23K gold on MDO plywood.

Designer: Eckert Morton Russo
Fabricator: Al Zanetti Sign Studios
               East Brunswick, New Jersey
Client: Eckert Morton Russo

The 4 × 4-ft. sign is painted on plywood.

◄

Designer: Roy McFaddin
Fabricator: Roy McFaddin, Inc.
               Independence, Oregon
Client: Roy McFaddin

The demonstration case shows off a complete variety of techniques offered by Roy McFaddin.

Eckert
morton
Russo architects
A professional association & planners

North Brunswick, New Jersey 08902

Designer: Ed Carey
Fabricator: Carey & Fort Woodcarvers
               South Windham, Maine
Client: Sam Davidson, CPA

The sign is constructed of Sugar Pine and has been hand carved and gilded. The visor, quill and glasses are made of brade as is the rigging for the fishing boat. The bracket is fabricated out of hand-carved Maple.

Designer: Robin West Design
Fabricator: Robin West Design
               West Sacramento, California
Client: Dresbach Hunt-Boyer Mansion

The 4 × 8 ft. directory for a converted historical mansion, the custom moulding and plaster casts were required to match the window details on the building. Sign face is constructed of $\frac{3}{4}$-in. plywood with individual plaques of $\frac{1}{2}$-in. particle board.

Designer: Carol White
Fabricator: Paul J. White, Woodcarver
               East Sandwich, Massachusetts
Client: Wianno Place

The carved wood sign for an attorney and an accountant
is painted in muted earth tones.

Designer: Charles M. Crawford
Fabricator: Signs and Things
               Naples, Florida
Client: Fairwind Yacht Charters

Both sides of this Redwood sign were sandblasted to
three different depths for the boat, the sun, and the firm's
name. The water is hand carved in $\frac{3}{4}$-in. Redwood. "Great
Sailing Escapes" is sandblasted. The copy is variegated
gold leaf.

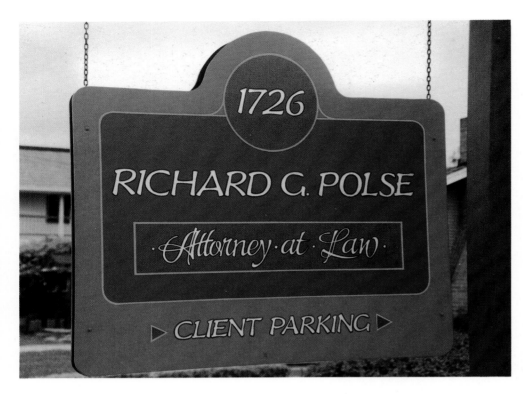

Designer: Carl Rohrs
Fabricator : Signs, Rohrs
Client: Richard Polse

The plywood sign was lettered with 23K surface gild.

Designers: Bob Morris, Tom Reaves
Fabricator: Signage Systems Company
              Hilton Head Island, South Carolina
Client: Bank of Beaufort

The sign company built the form for this sign, which was recessed into concrete. The sign was then sanded, sealed, and painted with liquid gold leaf.

Designer: Glennis Indreland
Fabricator: North Shore Sign Company
              Waukegan, Illinois
Client: American National Bank

The sign has a seamless aluminum face and routed letters with push-through clear acrylic backed with white acrylic. The eagles are of cast bronze. It is interiorly illuminated and mounted on a brick base that matches the building.

Designer: Melissa Byrd
Fabricator: Mississippi Electric Signs, Inc.
Client: Bank of Jackson

The sign faces were formed and embossed of acrylic with an aluminum cabinet, internally illuminated. The pole cover and trim were covered with acrylic filler and finish coat painted to match the bank building.

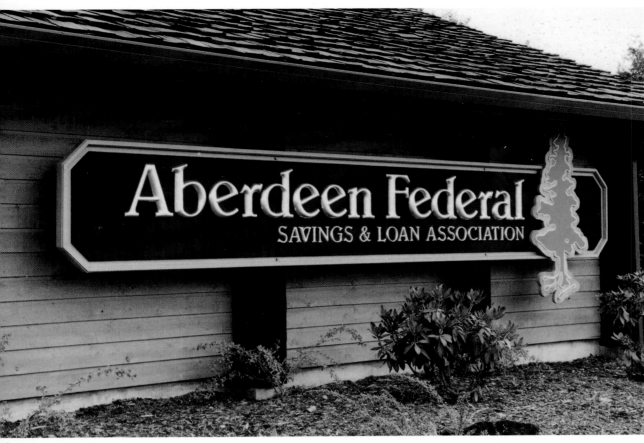

Designer: John F. Hannuakaine
Fabricator: John F. Hannuakaine Company
Tumwater, Washington
Client: Aberdeen Federal Savings & Loan
Association

The background is constructed Cedar and Fir with round-faced Pine letters with 23K gold leaf finish. The tree is sandblasted Redwood.

Designer: Neon Products Ltd.
Fabricator: Neon Products Ltd.
Vancouver, British Columbia, Canada
Client: Royal Bank

The cube displaying the corporate logo is painted on plastic, nonilluminated. The facia is a fully illuminated acrylic display.

Designer: Roger K. Smathers
Fabricator: Signs South
Greenville, South Carolina
Client: Greenville National Bank

This sign system for a bank used sandblasted clear Cedar.

Designer: Virgil Davis/Brown, Koby & Levingston
              Advertising
Fabricator: Scott Louviere Sign Company
              Lake Charles, Louisianna
Client: National Bank of Commerce

The bank's logo graphics were painted on the truck.

Designer: Heinz Prosch and Associates Designs, Inc.
              Coquitlam, British Columbia, Canada
Client: Yorkshire Trust

The free-standing sign identifies a bank.

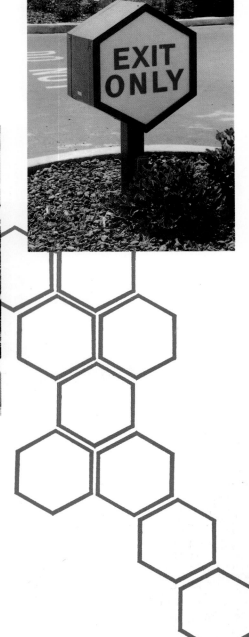

Designer: Bill Cawthorn
Fabricator: Comet Neon & Plastic Signs
              Escondido, California
Client: ENB

For this set of systems for a bank, the designers used metal cabinets with a textured finish. White and rust acrylic faces were used to match the main ID sign.

Designer: Daniel R. Dillon
Fabricator: Daniel R. Dillon Design Associates
                Cohoes, New York
Client: The Michaels Group

For a low key but formal appearance, this hand-carved
Redwood sign was painted forest green with 22K gold
leafed lettering.

Designers: Don Madsen, Larry Green
                Trammel Crow Company
                David Harding
                Pioneer Signs
Fabricator: Pioneer Signs
                Carrollton, Texas
Client: Xerox Corporation

The sign consists of a brushed aluminum box and posts,
with copy in bronze anodized cast aluminum.

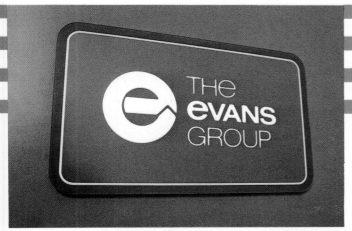

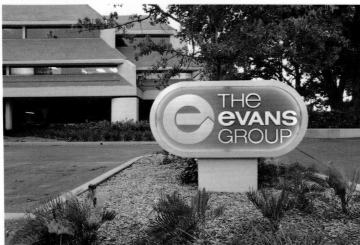

Designer: Kaiser Advertising, Inc.
Fabricator: Architectural Signage and Display
              Orlando, Florida
Client: The Evans Group

The main casing of the exterior sign is .062 aluminum painted gray; the logo and band are stainless steel. The interior sign is backed with white and rose neon.

4

Corporate Identification

The image that Corporate America wants to present is one of strength and durability. ''Massive,'' ''stable'' and ''balanced'' are adjectives that can often be used to describe the signs that help build and maintain the image of corporations. Many of the signs are literally constructed from ''a piece of the rock.'' Corporate America does not so much have a need for an individual sign as it has the desire to erect an enduring monument to celebrate its existence.

DESIGN
DESIGN
DESIGN
DESIGN
DESIGN

Fabricator: Neon Products Ltd.
Client: Consolidated Fastrate Transportation
          Group

The sculptured sign was fabricated in heavy-gauge aluminum with a baked enamel bronze finish, and mounted on a concrete plinth.

Designer: Claude Neon Federal
Fabricator: Claude Neon Federal
            Tulsa, Oklahoma
Client: MPSI Centre

The fabricated metal sign cabinet has radius corners sitting on a concrete base.

Designer: Cary W. Pampu
Fabricator: Blanchett Neon Ltd.
            Edmonton, Alberta, Canada
Client: Strathcona Refinery

Channel letters are mounted on Cedar and backed with neon illumination.

Designer: Jim Wittke
Fabricator: Valley City Sign Company
              Comstock Park, Michigan
Client: Howard Miller Clock Company

The 3 × 10-ft., double-faced anodized aluminum faces employ routed-out copy backed with yellow plastic. The cabinet frame is fabricated of aluminum angle iron construction. Filler material is brushed stainless steel.

Designer: State Sign Corporation
Fabricator: State Sign Corporation
              Orange, Texas
Client: Mony

The ground sign employs wooden stained letters set on an acrylic base.

Fabricator: CMR Sign & Lighting
Portland, Oregon
Client: Western Energy

The polycarbonate face was back-sprayed with gray, red, and white paint.

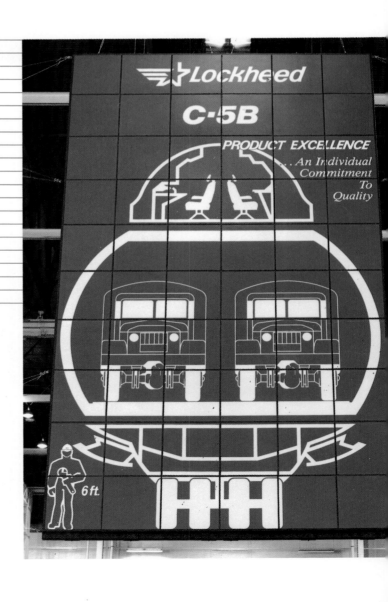

Designers: J. Minidis, N. Jack, M. Hucall
Fabricator: Industrial Illustrations
             Burbank, California
Client: Lockheed Plant #10

Each side of this 24 × 40-ft., free-suspended mural is comprised of sixty 4 × 4-ft. handpainted foamboard panels attached to the superstructure by hook-and-loop fasteners. By utilizing a grid/panel system, the supergraphics could be designed and installed more efficiently and with considerably less cost. The lightweight panels are changed in a matter of hours while the wood superstructure remains in place.

Designer: John F. Hannukaine
Fabricator: John F. Hannukaine
                Tumwater, Washington
Client: Capital Northwest Management
                Corporation

The sign is constructed of solid wood. All pieces have radius edges and oil finish. Most of the copy was applied by frisket paper which was cut and rolled on with enamel.

Designer: Michael Pasquarell Association
                Sydney, New South Wales, Australia
Fabricator: Macrographics
                Kingsgrove, New South Wales, Australia
Client: Rank Xerox

The front panel lettering is plated brass with reverse lettering behind the glass. The real panel is screen printed with a two-part mix in black to represent the Xerox copies of the original.

Designer: Sherry Snow
Fabricator: Comco
               San Diego, California
Client: Systech

This sign, measuring 7 ft. high and 5 ft. wide, is made of metal with a molded look. At night, the logo's blue on blue effect is created by $2\frac{1}{2}$-in. deep acrylic letters with blue neon reverse lighting.

Designer: Mark Baty
Fabricator: Baty Art + Sign, Inc.
Waukee, Iowa
Client: Economy Data Products

The sign is constructed with an aluminum pan background with cut-out aluminum letters, finished in automotive enamel.

Designer: Strategic Identities, Inc.
Fabricator: Talley Neon & Advertising
Richmond, Virginia

The three-sided structure is of fabricated metal with copy painted on two sides. The top panel has routed copy backed by illuminated acrylic. Bottom panels are removable.

Designer: Mike Johnson
Fabricator: Graphicon Corporation
                 Greensboro, North Carolina
Client: MSA

The sign is constructed of .080 aluminum with steel angle framing, and routed copy backed by $\frac{1}{8}$-in. white acrylic.

Designer: Concrete Monument:
                       Ehrlich-Rominger, Architects
                       Los Altos, California
Lettering Application: Clare Wild and Jeff Barnecut,
                       Sign Classics
Fabricator: Sign Classics, Inc.
                       California
Client: Cypress Semiconductor

The sign is a concrete monument with letters of $1\frac{3}{4}$-in. thick marine-grade ply with aluminum-leafed faces and blue edges. Letters and logo are mounted with pens and spacers.

Designer: Alice Lee
                Moretta & Sheehy Architects
                Chicago, Illinois
Fabricator: Arrow Sign, Company
                Chicago, Illinois
Client: Teradyne

The sign is made of a single, 18-ft.-long flat aluminum
plate and extrusion. There are no visible fastenings; all
corners and seams are continuous welded and ground
smooth. The letters are cut into the background and
backed with acrylic, and illuminated with metal halide
lamps.

Designer: Jerry Carpenter
Fabricator: W. Heath and Company
Dallas, Texas
Client: Aloe Vera

The sign is a fabricated metal cabinet with letters routed out and backed with bronze acrylic. The interior illumination is with halide lamps. The logo is flat plastic with colors sprayed on a second surface.

Designer: Christman Studios, Inc.
Fabricator: Christman Studios, Inc.
St. Louis, Missouri
Client: Olin

The brass sheeting was handcut and laminated over a wooden mold to form the corporate logo for use at a brass manufacturing plant. The sign is finished in clear epoxy.

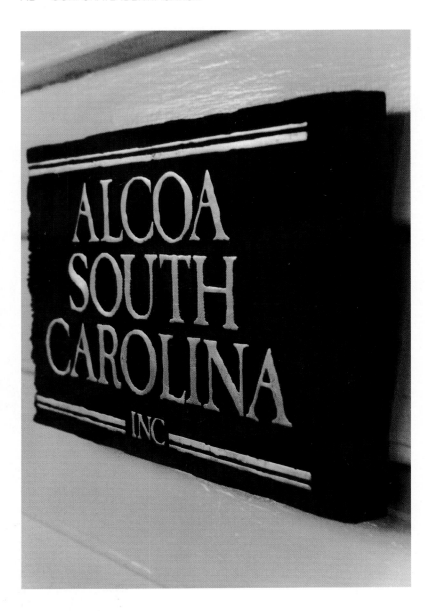

Designer: Lillian Nilsson
Fabricator: Classic Signs & Designs
               Beaufort, South Carolina

The sign is made of sandblasted 2-in. thick Redwood with an indigo stain. The lettering is 23K gold leaf, antiqued to complement the historic building the sign is attached to.

Designer: Michelle Zachiem
               Denver, Colorado
Fabricator: Colorado Woodsmiths, Inc.

Client: Estancia Primera

The 4 × 12-ft. double kiln-dried clearheart Redwood has a boxed frame. The Pine branch is sandblasted with individually cut-out plywood letters. The sign is finished with an exterior acrylic overcoat.

Designer: Neon Products, Ltd.
Fabricator: Neon Products, Ltd.
               Vancouver, British Columbia, Canada
Client: Nova: An Alberta Corporation

All seams and bolts of this sculpture were sanded and covered with four coats of high-gloss, brass-colored plastic paint. The routed copy is exterior illuminated.

Designer: Don Watt & Associates
Fabricator: Acralume Signs & Displays Ltd.
               Mississauga, Ontario, Canada
Client: Continental Bank

The free-standing, three-dimensional logo is approximately 15 ft. high and is manufactured and formed out of $\frac{1}{8}$-in. aluminum. There are no visible screws or bolts on this logo, which is cantilevered off its free-standing base.

Designer: Allan Sign Man Corporation
Fabricator: Allan Sign Man Corporation
               Plainview, New York
Client: Pergament

The "sign" consists of aluminum sheets wrapped around an iron frame. It was installed on a 3-in. pole. The artwork is handpainted to mimic the copy on an actual paint can label.

Designer: Roger K. Smathers
Fabricator: Signs South
                Greenville, South Carolina
Client: Goudelock

Letters and logo are constructed of foamboard attached to
a rock wall of a main reception area of an ad agency.
The cutouts and the wall have a blown stipple surface.
The sign is 4 ft. in diameter.

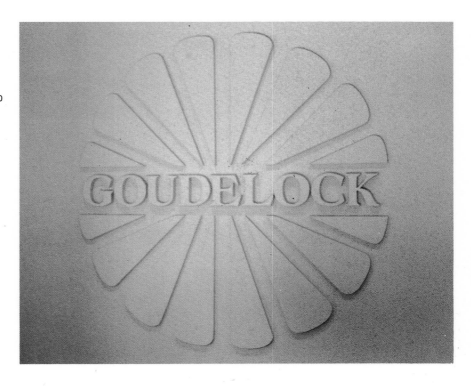

Designer: Dan Ward
Fabricator: Sign Force
                San Jose, California
Client: Eagle Computer

This is a sheet metal sign with an acrylic enamel finish.
The logo was stripped in and sprayed, the address hand
lettered.

5

Public Works

Public Works constitutes a broad base of community services which are funded either completely or partly by the government. Typical examples of these non-private sector projects include hospitals, airports, zoos and museums.

This chapter on Public Works present special problems to the environmental graphic designer, the one who is usually entrusted with the task of planning, programming and specifying graphic elements within an environment. These problems are not so much of designing proper identifications, as they are of keeping the traffic flowing. Directing masses of people efficiently through a maze of corridors requires careful placement of highly legible signs and pictograms. This, in turn, requires a thorough understanding of the facility, and how it operates.

The sheer number of signs needed by a facility such as a hospital or hotel can be extraordinary, literally thousands of signs which might have to be changed or replaced at a moment's notice. The sign systems developed by the environmental graphic designers must be flexible, and they must conform, by law, to certain standards such as those which protect the rights of the handicapped in public places.

In addition, with almost every project, comes its own special set of circumstances. For instance, Ad-Art Inc., Stockton, California recently provided 16,000 signs for the King Khalid International Airport in Saudi Arabia. As formidable as the actual volume of signs was, the unique aspect of this project was rooted in the customs of the Middle Eastern culture. All Arabic copy, it was decreed, had to be equal to or greater in mass to its English counterpart regardless of word imbalance.

Ad-Art did not divulge the total contract price, but it is not uncommon for projects of this type to run into the millions of dollars. With the number of complexes increasing and growing larger every day, seven figure contracts may very well become the rule—not the exception—for an industry on the rise.

DESIGN
DESIGN
DESIGN
DESIGN
DESIGN

VIRGINIA M. McCUNE
COMMUNITY
ARTS
CENTER
CROOKED TREE
ARTS COUNCIL

FOOTHILLS
HOSPITAL

Designer: D. & J. Marshall
               Calgary, Alberta, Canada
Fabricator: Hico Resources, Ltd.
Client: Foothills Hospital

Manmade sandstone, 20 ft. long by 9 ft. high, was
sandblasted to carve out the copy. The copy was then
painted in corporate colors. Three lamps provide indirect
nighttime illumination.

Designer: Bruce Janssen
Fabricator: The Wood Shop
              Boyne City, Michigan
Client: Arts Center

The double-sided Redwood sign is 7 × 5 ft. in dimension with a sandblasted face. Letters are both painted and gilded. The treetrunk and branches are constructed of handcarved Zebrawood. The handcarved leaves are made of Padauk wood; background area is gilded. The edge of the sign panel is wrapped in copper with a lacquer applied to retain the shine. All applied carvings are mounted from behind with screws. The sign identifies a 100-year-old Victorian church which is now an area arts center.

Designer: Bruce Janssen
Fabricator: The Wood Shop
              Boyne City, Michigan
Client: Arboretum

All natural materials were used in keeping with the natural setting of a lakeside restaurant. The two-sided Cedar sign is 10 × 5 ft. in dimension and utilizes Zebrawood, Bubinga, Padauk, and Walnut.

Designer: Robert H. Allen, Jr.
Fabricator: Andco Industries Corporation
              Greensboro, North Carolina
Client: Cape Fear Memorial Hospital

The skirt and sign faces are fabricated of aluminum set into extrusions with the individual letters routed and backed with fiberglass. The 12 × 4-ft. sign is finished with a charcoal-baked enamel and a gray matte skirt.

Designer: Gerard Ryan
Fabricators: Cherry Lane Studios, G. Ryan Design
             Toronto, Ontario, Canada
Client: Pickering Museum

The 4 × 6-ft. sign is double-sided and made from two
sections of Pine. The two sections were laminated
together, with exterior grade plywood sandwiched
in-between for added strength. The surface was painted
with a high gloss exterior enamel.

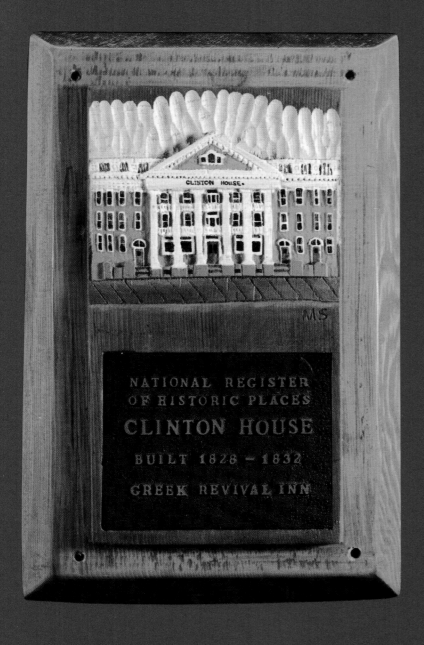

Designer: U. Romanoff & Associates
             Ithaca, New York
Fabricator: Shelley Signs
             Ithaca, New York
Client: National Register of Historic Places

This plaque for a landmark building was carved from
2-in.-thick White Pine, painted with acrylics, and sealed
with marine varnish. The inset plaque with lettering is
brass.

Designer: Kim Giordano
Fabricator: Creator's Touch, Inc.
Client: Lafayette House

This double-sided sign was hand-carved, the figures in
relief, the letters incised. The sign was then painted and
gold leafed. The pole is 6 × 6 steel square tubing
concealed by wood.

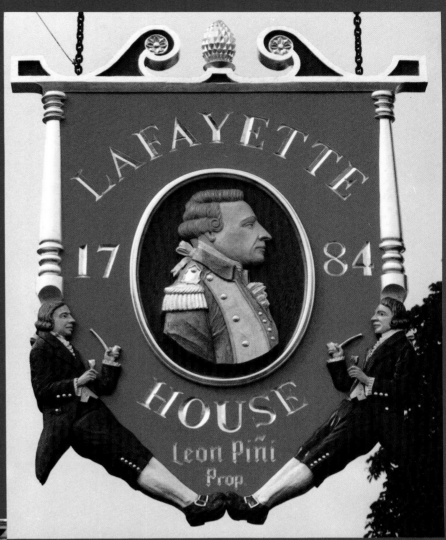

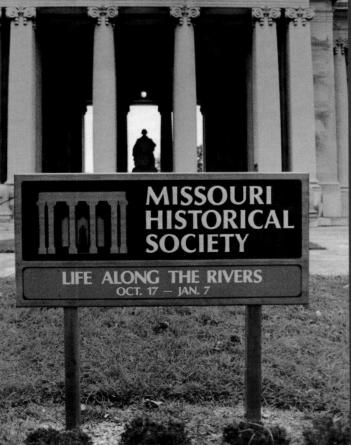

Designer: Christman Studios
Fabricator: Christman Studios
             St. Louis, Missouri
Client: Missouri Historical Society

This routed and sandblasted Redwood panel measures 3
ft. × 6 ft. × 2 in. thick. The letters are done in 23K
gold leaf. The lower panel is replaceable for special event
signs.

Designer: Artglo Sign Company
Fabricator: Artglo Sign Company
Columbus, Ohio
Client: Columbus Museum of Art

The double-faced ground sign is mounted on a tempered-glass base. The sculptured effect on the main identity complements several other sculptures on the front lawn of the Columbus Museum of Art.

Designer: Artglo Sign Company, Inc.
Fabricator: Artglo Sign Company, Inc.
Columbus, Ohio
Client: The Columbus Foundation

Designed to harmonize with the building's classic Victorian architecture, the sign consists of polished brass letters, a sheet metal face, and steel square, tube, and pipe welded and painted flat black.

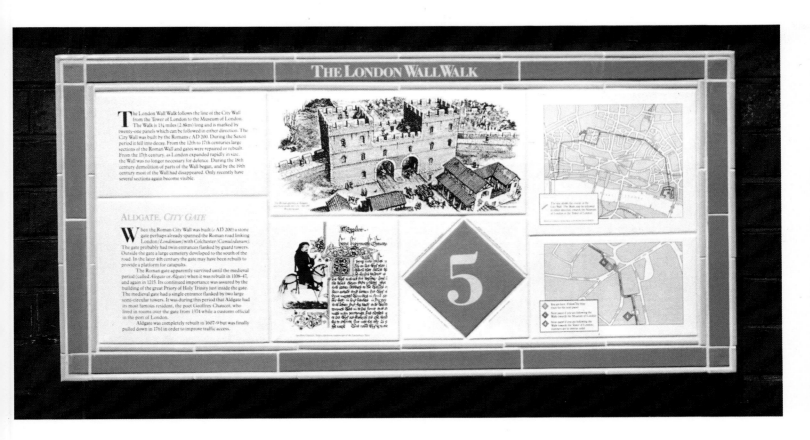

Designer: The Partners
             London, England
Fabricator: Maw and Company, Ltd.
             Stoke on Trent, England
Client: The London Wall Walk

Twenty-one ceramic tile signs follow the line of the old
City of London Wall. Each sign comprises over 60
hand-fired ceramic elements. These signs are positioned
from the Tower of London to the Museum of London.

Designers: Ad-Art, Inc., Bechtel Corporation
Fabricator: Ad-Art, Inc.
              Stockton, California
Client: King Khalid International Airport, Saudi
              Arabia

The system included internally illuminated directionals
and parking signs for both interior and exterior
installation in addition to a network of street, traffic and
highway signs. A total of 16,000 signs of all types were
required. The graphics were laser cut out of bronze vinyl
film and applied to specially mounted plastic faces. The
unique aspect in developing dual language graphics for
both English and Arabic copy was that due to "language
variables," the Arabic must always be equal to or greater
in "mass" than the English, regardless of word
imbalance.

Designer: Jay Cooke
Fabricator: Jay Cooke's Sign Shop
Stowe, Vermont
Client: Stowe School

This two-sided sign was made of Honduras Mahogany, measuring 4 × 6 ft. The letters were chip-carved and the illustration was handpainted in acrylic paints.

Designer: Karlsberger & Associates, Inc.
Fabricator: Karlsberger & Associates, Inc.
              Columbus, Ohio
Client: Health One

The primary identification sign has a quarry tile base and painted aluminum cap and three-dimensional letters. "Health One" and strip are reverse channel with neon illumination at night. Secondary signage is fabricated of painted aluminum and sub-surface painted Lexan. The directory is fabricated of routed Alucobond backed with painted acrylic.

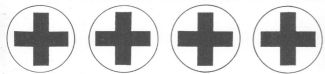

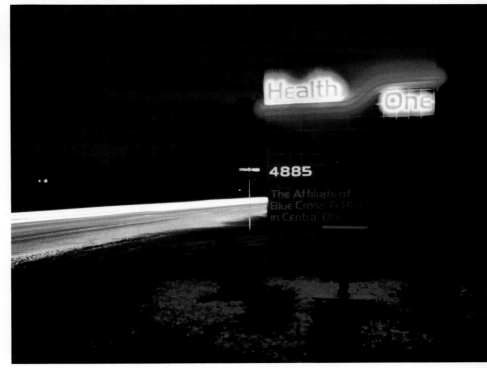

Designer: Bruce A. Daniels
                 Perkins and Will (architects)
                 Chicago, Illinois
Fabricator: **Tishman Construction of Arizona**
                 (general contractor)
Client: Tucson Medical Center

The concrete sign has been coated to recreate a
stucco-like appearance which characterizes so much of
the American West. The saguaro cactus, a redesigned
stylized logo for the medical center, was formed out of
foam, attached, and then coated on the concrete.

Designer: Donna Kite
Fabricator: Rustic Graphics
                 Roswell, Georgia
Client: Okefenokee Swamp Park

Designed for a theme park, the sandblasted signs are
done on 2-in.-thick Cedar stained with natural colors.

Designer: Joe Sonderman
               Charlotte, North Carolina
Fabricator: Graphic Systems International, Inc.
               Greensboro, North Carolina
Client: North Carolina Zoological Park

The ground-mounted topographic map and directory
provides pedestrian tour information at the North Carolina
Zoological Park. The relief map and the screen-printed
acrylic face were adapted to a custom component system.

Designer: Joe Sonderman
               Charlotte, North Carolina
Fabricator: Graphic Systems International, Inc.
               Greensboro, North Carolina
Client: North Carolina Zoological Park

The ground-mounted primary identification cluster is
composed of hand-sprayed aluminum columns adapted to
a custom support component system used throughout the
project.

Designer: Ben Kuzma
Fabricator: First Neon Sign and Service Company
                Cleveland, Ohio
Client: Cleveland Playhouse Square Center

Neon was chosen for the signage for Cleveland's theater center not only for its practicality but also for its inherent festive ambience. The lettering style was chosen from an old (circa 1930s) handbill, but the color (Voltan neo-blue pumped with neon gas) was chosen for its contemporary look. The State Theater sign has 12-in. high letters; all the other signs are 8 in. or less – all that was deemed necessary given the neon's high visibility factor.

Designer: Mark Faverman
Fabricator: Flying Colors, Inc.
              Boston, Massachusetts

The temporary banners stretch across the street.

Designer: Mark Faverman
Fabricator: Flying Colors, Inc.
              Boston, Massachusetts

The hanging banners add a touch of life to an open space.

Designers: Laura Rankin, Dan Sack, A. P. Ferulla ©
              Buffalo, New York
Fabricators: Eastern Signs, Central Rede Sign
              Company
              Buffalo, New York
Client: Elmwood Place

The tango dancers' project was commissioned by the
Buffalo Department of Community Development and is
intended to create a unique lighting design to attract
attention and stimulate business in Buffalo's Elmwood
area —an entertainment mecca. The tango dancers cross
fade — one image dissolving into the next. A 1,200-ft.
band of blue neon (not shown) complements the mural
and fronts the façade of those Buffalo businesses which
support the project.

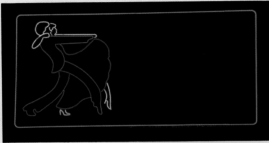

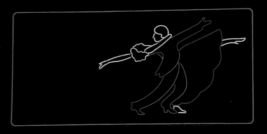

Designers: Bob Bond/Van Nuys, California,
               Beverly Hills Motor Car Society
Fabricator: Bob Bond, California Rehabilitation
               Center
Client: Beverly Hills Motor Car Society

The 1928 Ahrens Fox Fire Engine has been meticulously
restored by Bob Bond, a pinstriper who worked with a
group of model prisoners from the California
Rehabilitation Center. The restoration actually occurred
over a 6–8 month period at the prison.

Designer: David Harding
Fabricator: A Sign of Excellence
               Carrollton, Texas
Client: The Poster Gallery

The client wanted a showcard to announce his new
location. It was decided to make the showcard look like a
poster. A real poster was used, with the words ''Coming
Soon'' and ''The Poster Gallery'' were cut on a sign maker
and mounted on the glass face covering the poster.

Designer: Hansen Lind Meyer, P.C.
Orlando, Florida
Fabricator: ETM Graphics
Burnsville, Minnesota
Client: University of Iowa Hospital

Flat-painted and three-dimensional cartoon characters ease anxiety levels in a children's area of a hospital. Some computer-painted murals were incorporated.

6

Real Estate

Signs for Real Estate businesses in addition to identifying property also try to create an image and give a sense of the place. Whether they are used to mark an office complex, a residential development, or individual buildings, well designed signs add an element that help set the mood.

This chapter contains a wide variety of signs. Some identify commercial properties, others mark the location of residential areas—all provide inspiration and ideas.

DESIGN
DESIGN
DESIGN
DESIGN

Designers: Craig Hanson, Barham-Fancher,
               Tony Vigliotti
               Tyler, Texas
Fabricator: Cavanaugh Art & Design
               Flint, Texas
Client: Atelier Office Condominiums

The 3 × 16-ft. sign is made of $\frac{1}{4}$-in.-thick laminated
ivory acrylic. The transparent, buffed-red acrylic letters
are mounted on height spacers over a brass rod design.

Designer: Charles Rouse
Fabricator: Rouse Sign & Graphics
               Vista, California
Client: Camino de Vista

The sign consists of matte-finish case metal letters
mounted in relief on a section of laminated beam similar
to the building material, sandblasted and stained to
match the building.

Designer: G. Ryan Design, Inc.
Fabricator: G. Ryan Design, Inc.
Toronto, Ontario, Canada
Client: Heathwood

The entrance of a subdivision consists of a set of brick gates with sandblasted sandstone slabs. Just one of many signs in the total system, the Heathwood sales office design was voted the best presentation in Canada for 1982 by a committee of Canadian home builders.

Client: Ridge Court Condominiums

The 4 × 7-ft. MDO plywood sign is painted in gold
bronze with a black outline. The border is fire red and
imitation gold. The copy "Ridge Court" and the row of
Victorian houses have been varnished.

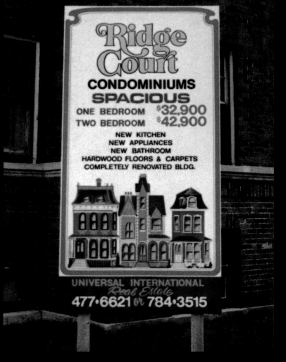

Designer: Joe Sonderman
                 Joe Sonderman, Inc.
                 Charlotte, North Carolina
Client: Office Complex

The multi-colored cluster of signs are mounted to a
pedestrian deck area within a planned community
shopping complex. The painted metal poles have
screen-printed copy and graphics.

Designer: Tom Graboski Associates
Coconut Grove, Florida
Fabricator: Melweb Signs, Inc.
Ft. Lauderdale, Florida
Client: Office at Bay Point

This exterior building sign is 8 ft. high and consists of a
routed face with internal illumination. The logo was
custom designed.

Designers: Jerry O'Quinn (sign), Brooks Kennedy
(logo, Van Laan & Associates)
Fabricator: Graphicon Corporation
Greensboro, North Carolina
Client: Park Center

This sign combines radius corners with vertical reveals
and earth tones of bronze and orange stripes. The sign
cabinet is made of .080 aluminum. The routed copy is
illuminated by T-12 high-output lamps.

Designer: David Hamby
Fabricator: Action Sign Company
               Lenoir, North Carolina
Client: Elk River

The sandblasted Cedar sign features a stained glass
background.

Designer: Taylor Group
               Dallas, Texas
Fabricator: Colorado Woodsmiths, Inc. of Texas
               Richardson, Texas
Client: Mallard Cove

The 4 × 4-ft. handcarved kiln-dried clearheart Redwood
sign is mounted on Redwood posts, stained and painted
with an acrylic coat.

Designer: Mike Jackson
Fabricator: Jackson Signs
Moore, Oklahoma
Client: Lakeside Office Estates

Painted wood sign on MDO plywood.

Designer: Christman Studios
Fabricator: Christman Studios
St. Louis, Missouri
Client: Deer Field

Carved pictorial and lettering is in Poplar; framing and posts are made of rough-sawn Cedar. Letters are 23K gold leafed; deer scene is oil-stained.

Designer: G. Ryan Design, Inc.
Fabricator: G. Ryan Design, Inc.
              Toronto, Ontario, Canada
Client: The Marshall Estates

The signs for these estate homes were sandblasted from 2-in. Canadian White Pine and painted with exterior-grade enamel paint. ▶

Designer: Reed Design Associates
Fabricator: Reed Design Associates
              Madison, Wisconsin
Client: Fire Station Offices

Designed for an old firehouse that was renovated and converted to office space, the polished bronze sign is etched and filled in with red and black paint.

Designer: Starla Dungan
Fabricator: Don Bell & Company
              Port Orange, Florida
Client: Silversands

A V-shaped sign structure of poured concrete with stucco finish. It is flat cut out of $\frac{1}{4}$-in polished aluminum copy, mounted to a raised stucco background. Externally illuminated by floodlights.

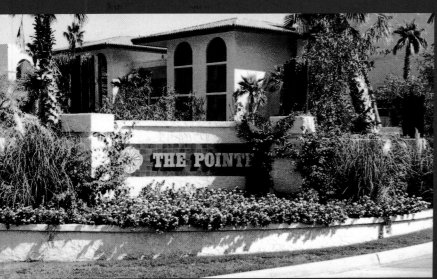

Designer: Larry McKitchens
Fabricator: GDC Sign Studio
             Phoenix, Arizona
Client: The Pointe Resort

Blue Italian ceramic tile was inserted into this stucco wall, and then the logo was sandblasted. The $1\frac{1}{2}$-in. reverse pan letters are chrome plated.

Designer: Glenn Robbins
Fabricator: Habitat, Inc.
               Tempe, Arizona
Fabricator: Water Works Home

The sign consists of kiln-dried Cedar, 12-in. copper pipe, and 11½ baffles to give the special water effect. Blue metal shelves were added at the base to give the splashing effect.

Designer: Fulton Advertising
Ft. Lauderdale, Florida
Fabricator: Melweb Signs, Inc.
Ft. Lauderdale, Florida
Client: Spectrum Office Building

The sign consists of an all-aluminum frame with
non-illuminated, stainless-steel faces which are 7 ft. 2 in.
square. The overall height is 14 ft. Copy and graphics
appear on all six sides of the cube.

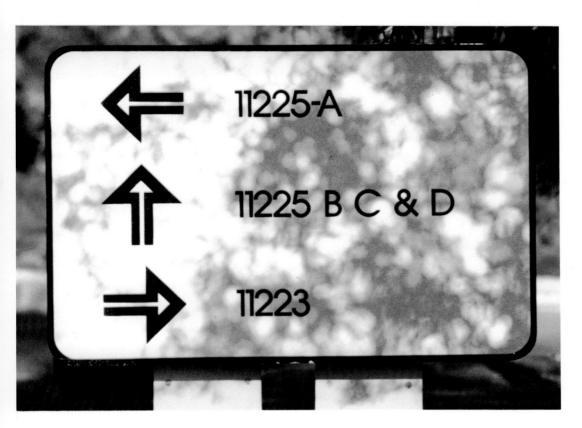

Designer: Larry Keese
           Graphics Hardware Company
           Phoenix, Arizona
Fabricator: SmithCraft Manufacturing Company
            Phoenix, Arizona
Client: Lincoln Centre

A complete sign system for a 140,000-sq.-ft. office complex, the signs consist of polished, stainless and chrome-plated steel, anodized aluminum, and reflective materials. The primary identification is constructed of stainless steel with a brightly polished finish, routed and acrylic-backed letters, and a double in-line border all mounted on a concrete base. The direction sign is satin anodized aluminum plate mounted on aluminum supports with 3-in. radius bends and blind anchor bolts set on acrylic, and a concrete base which matches the building. Inserts are gold anodized aluminum bars with pressure-sensitive vinyl letters. Suite identifications employ pressure-sensitive vinyl copy on brushed aluminum.

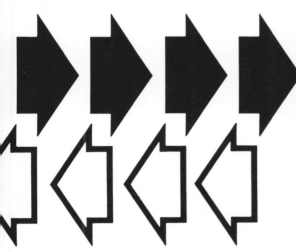

Designer: Larry Keese
             Graphics Hardware Company
             Phoenix, Arizona
Fabricator: SmithCraft Manufacturing Company
             Phoenix, Arizona
Client: Lincoln Centre

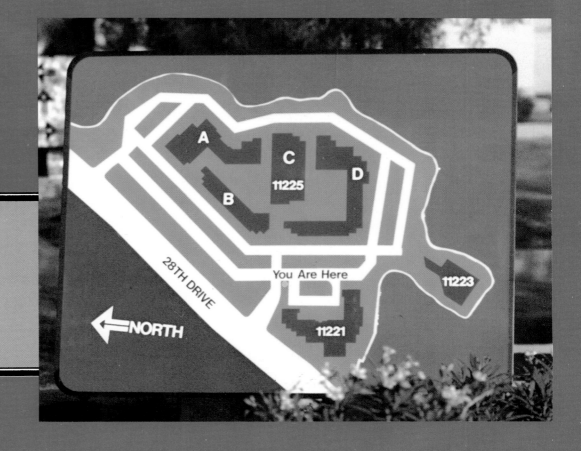

Designer: Michel Lajeunesse
Fabricator: Creation Vieil Art
               Granby, Quebec, Canada
Client: Les Charron

An old Cedar post was sculpted to appear antique. The name was sandblasted. Dyes and oiled enamels were wiped in to give an "old paint feeling."

Designer: Cia Houston-Hobbs
               Jacksonville Beach, Florida
Fabricator: Fibremart Designs, Inc.
               Ponte Vedra Beach, Florida
Client: Courtney South Beach

The construction sign identifies a beach project. The logo design, name concept, and signs were done by Fibremart.

Designer: Port Authority of New York and New
               Jersey
Fabricator: Frank Torrone & Sons, Inc.
               Staten Island, New York
Client: World Trade Center

The 5 × 20-ft. sign was manufactured from steel channel iron and converted with $\frac{1}{8}$-in. steel plate with stencil-cut and acrylic copy. The support base was manufactured from $\frac{1}{2}$-in. steel plate and $\frac{3}{8}$-in. steel walls then bolted to a concrete slab 4 ft. below grade.

World Trade Center

THE PORT AUTHORITY OF NY & NJ

WINDOWS ON THE WORLD
107th FLOOR RESTAURANT

Designer: Steve Mysse
Fabricator: Sign and Design
                Billings, Montana
Client: Creekside at the Homestead

Exterior tenant ID was silkscreened on beige
acrylic, mounted on concrete monuments.

Designer: D. I. Design + Developmental
                Consultants, Inc.
                Baltimore, Maryland
Fabricators: Brad Jirka Designers and
                Cork Marschesci
                The American School of Neon,
                Minneapolis, Minnesota
                Nordquist Sign Company,
                Minneapolis, Minnesota
Client: Riverplace

The sign is constructed of two, 9 × 24-ft. sections. The
glass work ranges anywhere from 10–15mm. thick neon.
Animation gives motion to the Riverboat's paddlewheel,
water, smoke and flag.

Fabricator: Bell Neon Sign Company
Philadelphia, Pennsylvania
Client: One Reading Center

A 1,000-ft. edge of blue neon ascends from curb to penthouse and highlights the border on three of the buildings four sides. Seemingly suspended in space, the columns of light give vertical dimension to the illuminated nighttime facade. Photo © Peter Olson.

Designer: Dick Leonard
Wood, Cohen, Leonard, & Busch
Tampa, Florida
Fabricator: Crystal Graphics, Inc.
Tampa, Florida
Client: Huntington Subdivision

The logo was completely handcut from a solid sheet of
½-in.-thick naval brass. The 30 × 96-in. sign was
polished to a high gloss and then sealed with acrylic
polyurethane. The logo is stud mounted.

Designer: Colorado Woodsmith, Inc.
Denver, Colorado
Fabricator: Colorado Woodsmith, Inc.
Client: Iron Horse Resort

Routed and cut metal was inserted into a stone structure
measuring 3 × 6 ft.

Designer: Bruce Janssen
Fabricator: The Wood Shop
 Boyne City, Michigan
Client: Lakehouse Condominiums

This handcarved solid Mahogany sign is 3 ft. wide, 2 ft. 4 in. high, and has a thickness ranging from 2 to 3 $\frac{1}{2}$ in. The sign is painted with acrylic, and the letters consist of 23K gold leaf.

Designer: Parker Sign Company, Inc.
 West Des Moines, Iowa
Fabricator: Parker Sign Company, Inc.
Client: Private Residence

The 3 × 6-ft. ground sign is made of fiberglass.

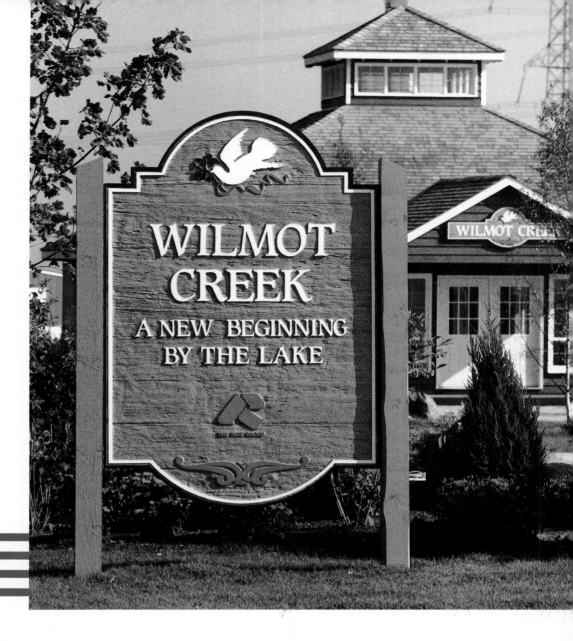

Designer: G. Ryan Design, Inc.
Fabricator: G. Ryan Design, Inc.
              Toronto, Ontario, Canada
Client: Wilmot Creek

All signs were sandblasted in 2-in.-thick Canadian White Pine. The background color is a flat blue to give the signs a weathered look. The letters and border were painted with high gloss enamel to provide a good contrast with the flat finish.

Designer: Joe Sonderman; Inc.
            Charlotte, North Carolina
Fabricator: Routed Signs, Inc.
            Ocala, Florida
Client: Millpond Park Developers

The dual-post Redwood structure supports a single-face,
screen-printed panel.

Designer: Tampa Outdoor Graphics, Inc.
Fabricator: Tampa Outdoor Graphics, Inc.
            Tampa, Florida
Client: Bay West Commerce Park

The cube sign is backlit and constructed of routed
aluminum. The secondary ID and the post/panel signs are
fabricated of aluminum with dimensional graphics.

Designer: Mike Smallwood
Fabricator: Signs of Yesteryear
               Austin, Texas
Client: Heritage Oaks

The wood portion of the structure consists of 4-in.-thick rough Cedar planks. Lettering is incised $\frac{1}{2}$ in. and stained with oils.

Designer: Betsy Harris
Fabricator: Freedom Signs
               Santa Barbara, California
Client: Cabrillo Bathhouse and East Beach Grill

This double-face sign includes sandblasted ceramic and quarry tile encased in a double frame of 1 × 2-in. and 1 × 6-in. clearheart Redwood. It is mounted with ¼-in. steel frames on 6 × 6-in. routed Redwood posts. The frame and posts of the 39 × 66-in. sign is finished with a solid-body stain to match the building's trim colors. The inset quarry tile matches the design tiles of the building. The lettering is unfinished clay showing through the blasted glaze.

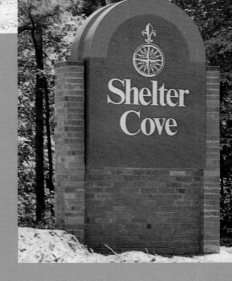

Designer: Joe Sonderman, Inc.
              Charlotte, North Carolina
Fabricator: Talley Neon & Advertising
              Richmond, Virginia
Client: Woodlake

"Woodlake" sign is metal with routed copy backed by
illuminated acrylic; individual neighborhood signs are
metal panels with painted copy.

Designer: Bill Ollinger
Fabricator: Woodcarver Designs Ltd.
              Mansfield, Ohio
Client: Sherwood Forest

The pictorial was sandblasted in four depths on this $6\frac{1}{2}$ × 4-ft. Western Red Cedar sign. The unicorn was then airbrushed, and the background stained in various shades.

Designer: Perry Pawley
Fabricator: Environmental Graphics
              Hilton Head Island, South Carolina
Client: Ocean Walk Villas

The sign was sandblasted out of clearheart Redwood panels. The gilded logo is mounted to a structure made of block and stucco with Cedar planters attached. The special feature is a fountain system designed into the center of the sign with a reservoir and pump underneath.

Designer: John Luttman
Fabricator: John Luttman, Woodcarver
                Wayne, Pennsylvania
Client: Sugar Knoll

Carved from South American Mahogany, this sign measures 3 ft. 4 in. × 4 in. × 2½ in. The wood is colored with oil stains and paints, while the letters are topped with 23K gold leaf. The lettered piece was set into a slide groove and was then bolted.

Designer: Gal Holliday
Fabricator: April Day Studio, Inc.
                Columbia, Maryland
Client: Hyde Park Walk

The 12 × 25-ft. double-sided street sign has screen-printed letters and logo set on $\frac{5}{8}$-in. MDO plywood. There were approximately 20 named street signs for this Huntington Townhouse development in Waldorf, Maryland.

Designer: Slater Associates
                Columbia, Maryland
Fabricator: April Day Studio, Inc.
                Columbia, Maryland
Client: Bryant Gardens

The 39 × 67-in. sign is painted on $\frac{5}{8}$-in. MDO background with screened-on lettering. The logo cut-out has been applied to picket fence directly for a condominium project.

SIGN
SIGN
SIGN
SIGN
SIGN
SIGN
SIGN
SIGN
SIGN

7

Experimental Work

The words "Commercial artist" have never really fit comfortably together. Art is beauty and truth, form and function. The one entrusted with its safeguarding, the artist, ideally is an individual free to create for a world which may accept, reject, or ignore the vision. Somehow, it seems unfair that the word "commercial" should ever act as its modifier. Here's a word which often suggests the opposite of art. In a commercialistic universe, truth too often means "hype," individualism gives way to socialization and freedom of expression steps aside in deference to mass marketing.

No wonder so many commercial artists find it difficult straddling the fence which splits the two words. As one ad agency executive once wrote: "It's not easy pursuing God and mammon both at the same time."

In this chapter on Experimental Work, a handful of commercial artists have found a way. The commercial aspects of their craft have been subjugated to its artistic demands. Most of the work appearing in this chapter was done more to please the artist than the client. As a result, the majority of the designs pictured are not really signs at all—at least not in the traditional sense of identifying a good or a service or making an announcement.

This does not mean the "experiments" shown here are out of context with this book . Take a look at some of Bill Concannon's work at Aargon Neon in Benicia, California. Among other activities, it's been Concannon's "art" to construct miniature movie sets for such films as Francis Ford Coppola's "One From The Heart." Working closely with Larry Albright, a professor at the Institute of Eternal Light, Concannon has constructed a scaled down version of the sign capital of the world: Las Vegas. The works of Concannon and Albright are not so much for a client as they are for a patron, for they are commissioned.

Jeff Greene, from EverGreene Painting Studios in New York City is in a similar position. He became a full-time muralist, an offshoot of his earlier work as a pictorialist for a billboard company. He has experimented with a technique called trompe l'oeil, a French word meaning "to fool the eye." Greene's trompe l'oeil technique lives up to its definition. His sense of perspective is unfaltering. On a once lifeless wall, he brings life. From any distance more than a few feet, his pictorials appear real.

The technique has proved popular. The dozen or so muralists at EverGreen Painting Studios work only by referral these days. Meanwhile, the company's client list reads like an address book of Corporate America.

Greene is just one of several in this chapter who have found a market to keep their art alive. Christian Schiess, a neon sculptor from the Academy of Art College and an artist-in-residence at San Francisco's acclaimed Exploratorium, probably found the going a bit tough starting out, but gradually, his studies of the kinetic nature of light has found some financial backing. Due to the artistic success of *Lumens*—his first film—Schiess received a grant from the American Film Institute. Subsequently, a higher-budgeted sequel was made, *Luminauts*, followed by a third film *Calyx* and a fourth *Ignus Ex Machina*: *Fire from the Machine*. The films, as well as some of Schiess' other "viewer-responsive" experiments with neon, alter our perception of light and color.

All of the aforementioned artists—as well as most of the others appearing in this chapter—have found the energy and time to pursue their dreams regardless of the impending commercial success or failure of their work. That for the most part, they've been successful on both levels—the commercial and the artistic—is a fairly optimistic endorsement for all those thinking of doing a little experimenting on their own.

DESIGN
DESIGN
DESIGN
DESIGN
DESIGN

Designer: City Lights Neon
Fabricator: City Lights Neon
              Cincinnati, Ohio

The use of imported Bromo-blue, ruby red, emerald green, and coated Noviol gold glass, mix to create white light at the seating level and magenta at the eye level. The lamp unit is $7\frac{1}{2}$ ft. tall and installed in a Bromo-blue glass vase.

Client: Playboy Club
              Chicago, Illinois

The possibilities of laser projection are now a reality as witnessed by this graphic against the Playboy building in Chicago.

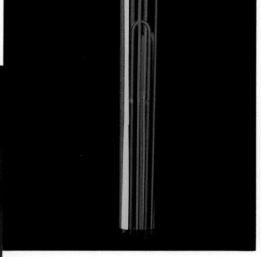

Designers: Larry Albright, Bill Concannon
Fabricator   Larry Albright/Sculptor, Bill Concannon
              Venice and Benicia, California
Client: One from the Heart

Larry Albright and Bill Concannon collaborated on this miniature neon film set for Francis Ford Copolla's "One from the Heart." The tubing for the set measures only 2mm.

Designer: Terry Boyle
Fabricator: City Lights Neon
                Cincinnati, Ohio
Client: Pam & Tom Kirchner (private collection)

The drawing on the left is a copy of a Matisse pen and
ink. The drawing on the right has been transposed and
altered for effect by Terry Boyle. The neon is turquoise,
pumped with neon and argon mercury gases. The neon,
which is wrapped around a paintbrush, is reliefed off the
surface of the drawing.

Designer: Christian Schiess
Fabricator: Christian Schiess
               Academy of Art College
               San Francisco, California

An experimental piece constructed of inflated vinyl, wire,
and neon.

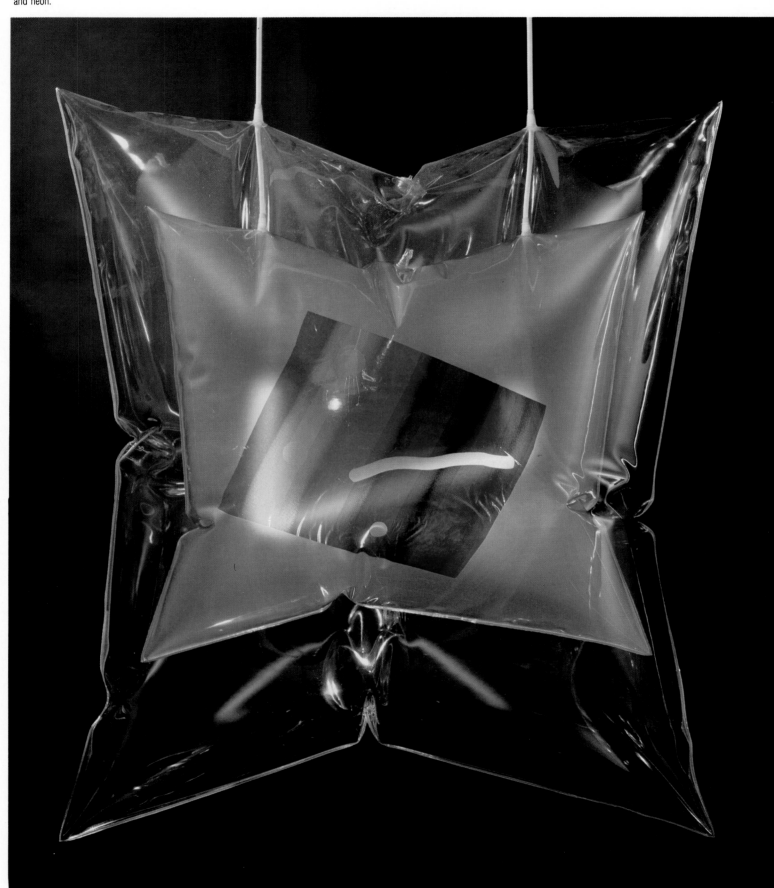

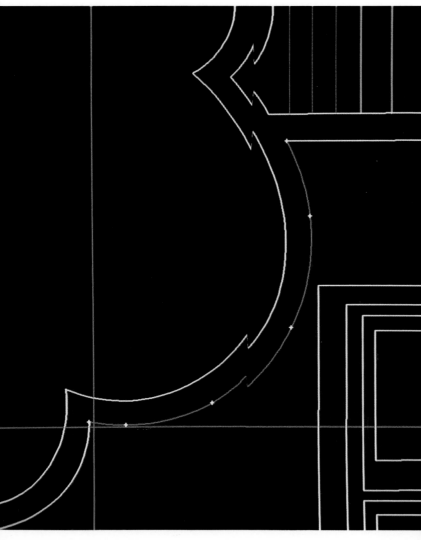

Designer: Vomela Corp.
Fabricator: Vomela Corp.
Minneapolis, Minnesota

Computer-aided design is now a reality in the sign industry. The operator inputs various coordinates (white dots) and the computer automatically draws a perfect arc (blue curved line). The resulting design graphic is then translated as a pattern for computerized cutting.

Designer: Christian Schiess
Fabricator: Christian Schiess
Academy of Art College
San Francisco, California
Client: Pink Light Rope (1980)

The 50-ft. pink light rope is 1 in. in diameter and is constructed of vinyl, dye, oil, wire, and neon glass.

Designer: T. Oestreicher © 1982
Fabricator: Neon Neon
San Francisco, California

The outline of neon men is 10 × 10 ft. in dimension.

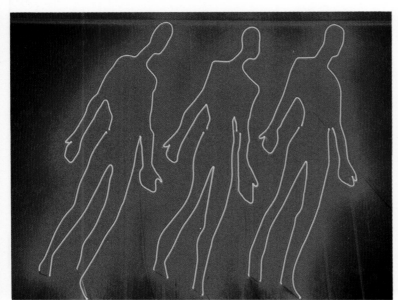

Designers: John Forbes/Bonny Doon Art Glass,
             Bruce Suba/Suba Neon
Fabricator: Suba Neon
             Santa Cruz, California
Client: Bonny Doon Art Glass

When John Forbes, proprietor of Bonny Doon Art Glass, desired to "put something really outrageous on my hot rod," he collaborated with Bruce Suba of Suba Neon. After several months of "relentless experiments," the two came up with these neon sparkplug wires.

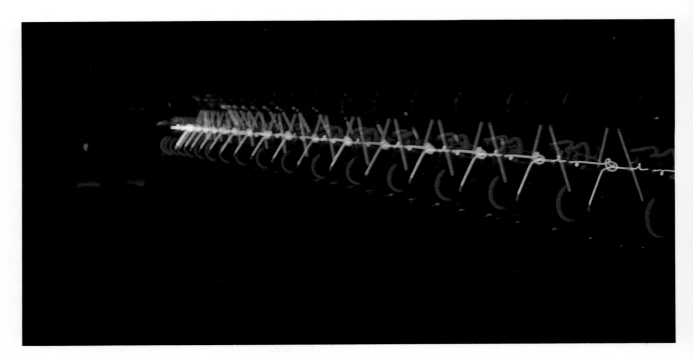

Designers: John Forbes/Bonny Doon Art Glass,
               Bruce Suba/Suba Neon
Fabricator: Suba Neon
               Santa Cruz, California
Client: Bonny Doon Art Glass

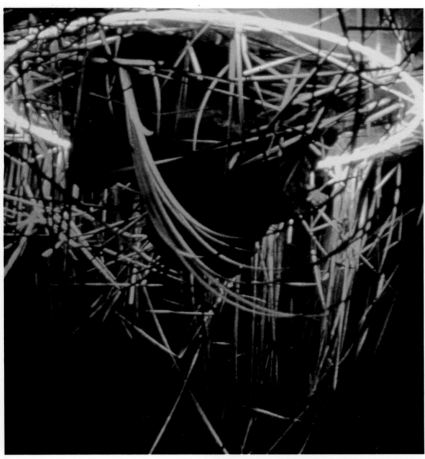

Designer: Christian Schiess
Fabricator: Christian Schiess
              Academy of Art College
              San Francisco, California
Client: #4-Fire/Water series

Mercury-argon tubing is set in water in this
5 × 5 × 5-ft. neon sculpture. Schiess is reportedly the
first to make neon work under water. This was done by
first coating the electrodes in a liquid state, then placing
plastic shields over the ends and injecting them with
silicone. The project is one of four which Schiess
conceived that involved the combining of the traditional
opposing elements — earth, wind, fire, and water.

Designer: Janna Longacre
Fabricator: Joseph P. Upham
              New York, New York
Client: Told!

Luminous krypton gas, glass, porcelain, and wood
combine in this 24 × 24 × 24-in. display.

Designer: Eric E. Pohl
Fabricator: Yerexneon, Inc.
               Scarborough, Ontario, Canada
Client: Bi-plane sculpture.

The bi-plane is approximately 20 × 20 × 9 in. with a
96-in vapor trail. A bi-plane is suspended about 4 ft.
from the ceiling. Pohl comments that his interest in the
graphic possibilities of three-dimensional surfaces is
always growing. Another dimension adds variety to the
viewing angles, in contrast with most graphic work which
suffers from anything by a dead-front view.

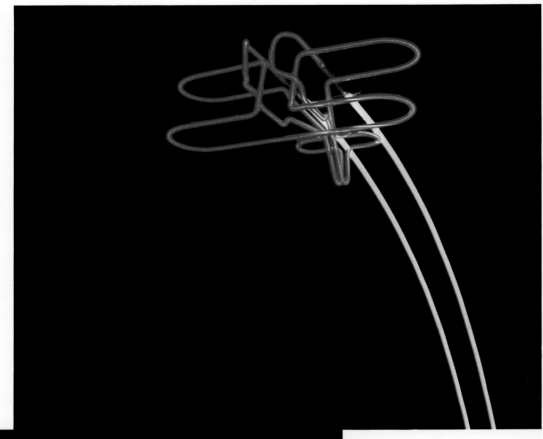

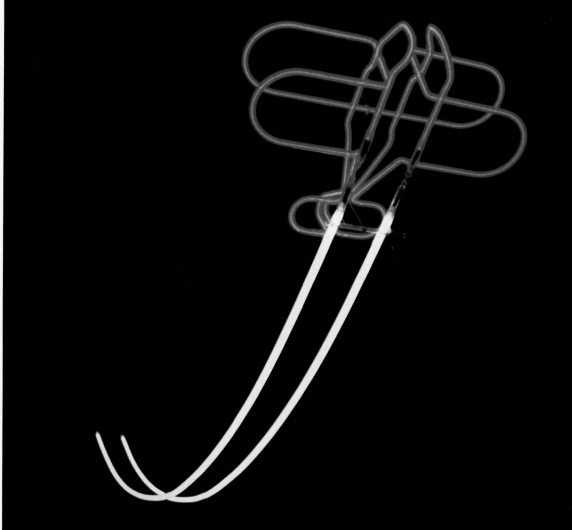

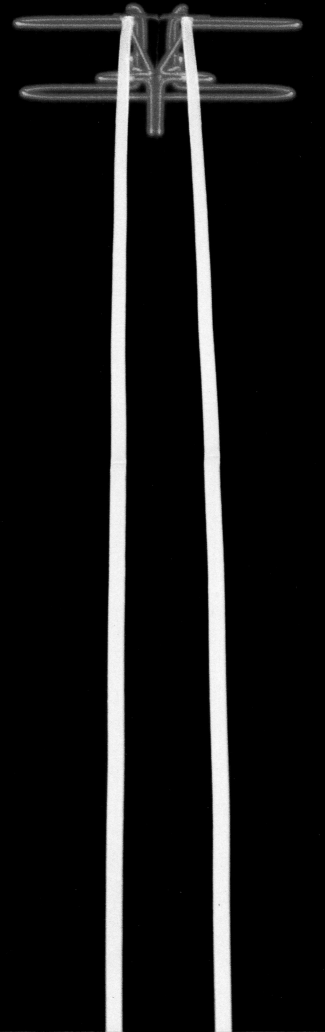

Designer: Ad Laser
Fabricator: Ad Laser
San Marcos, California

Laser art appears a possibility on the horizon.

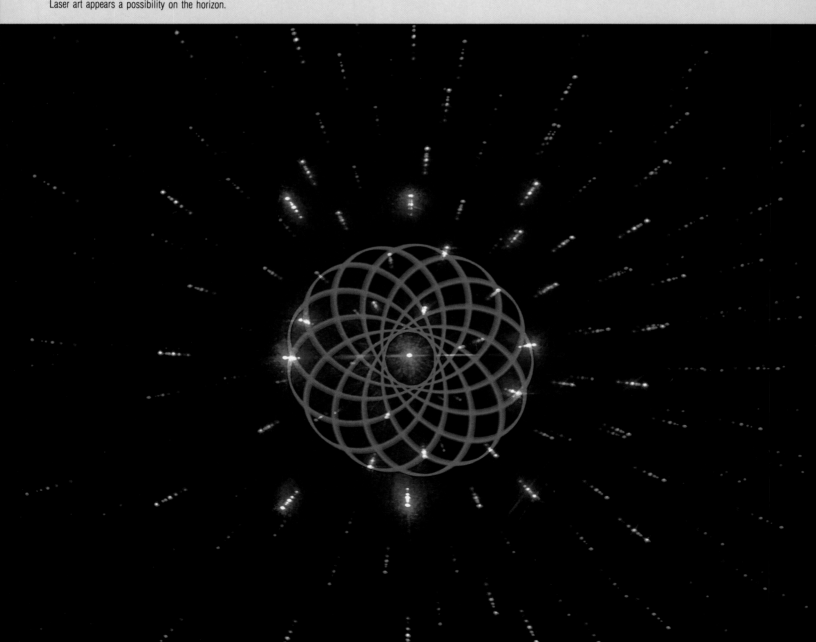

Designer: Bill Concannon
Fabricator: Aargon Neon
               Benicia, California
Client: Pink Blue Flasher

Created in 1980, the "Pink Blue Flasher's" center tube is 18mm glass spliced into 7mm sections which are filled with a combination of mercury vapor and neon, then "flashed" with a high voltage animator. "It's unusual," notes Concannon, "because it's a clear tube with two colors, the pink staying in the 7mm sections and the blue in the 18mm."

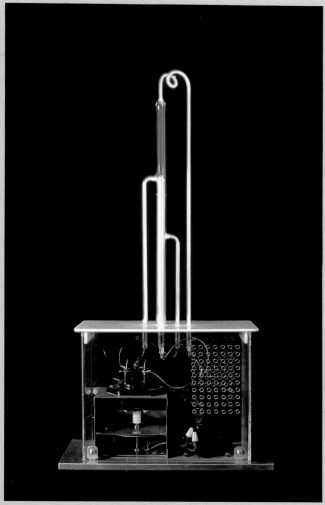

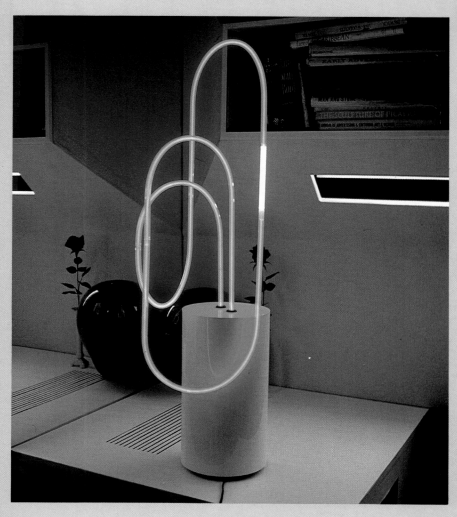

Designer: John Tanaka
Fabricator: John Tanaka
               New York, New York

Neon sculpture for a private residence .

Designer: Tom Hayden
Fabricator: EverGreene Painting Studios, Inc.
                New York, New York
Client: Glass Farmhouse

A cooperative residential renovation in New York City.

Designer: EverGreene Painting Studios, Inc.
Fabricator: EverGreene Painting Studios, Inc.
                New York, New York
Client: Bankers Trust Haborside Building, New
                Jersey

Trompe L'oeil panoramic view of the Manhattan skyline
created for employee's cafeteria.

Designer: EverGreene Painting Studios, Inc. ➤
Architect: Roy Rosembaum
Fabricator: EverGreene Painting Studios, Inc.
                New York, New York
Client: Paddlewheel Casino in Las Vegas

Trompe L'oeil mural created for Paddlewheel Casino in
Las Vegas.

ATRIUM FACADE

EVERGREEN'S NYC

E.ABREU. S.LAZARUM.

APPROVED BY O.T.CARR

PHASE 2

Designer: EverGreene Painting Studios, Inc.
Fabricator: EverGreene Painting Studios, Inc.
               New York, New York
Client: The Oliver T. Carr Company

A 125 × 23-ft. construction fence, painted in
water-based paint, has Trompe L'oeil peek-through,
showing the back of the architect's blueprint where the
wall is "pinned back."

Designer: EverGreene Painting Studios, Inc.
Fabricator: EverGreene Painting Studios, Inc.
               New York, New York
Client: The Limited Company

This decorative construction barricade created for The Limited Company has Trompe L'oeil architecture, bronze stenciling, and lettering.

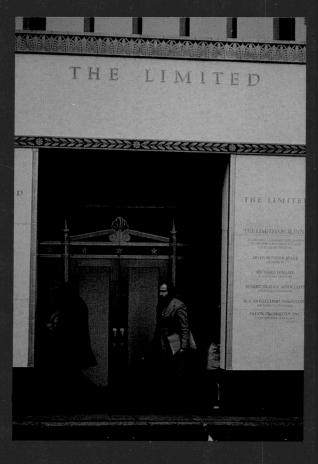

Designer: Peter Saari
                Corporate Art Directions
Fabricator: EverGreene Painting Studios, Inc.
                New York, New York
Client: Crown Building

Trompe L'oeil ornaments, murals, faux marble, and stencils form the vaulted ceiling of the Crown Building Lobby in New York City.

Designer: Christian Schiess
Fabricator: Christian Schiess
               San Francisco, California
Client: Lumens (1980)

In 1980, Schiess developed this "light suit" for the
movie, "Lumens." The experimental film, which was
produced by Schiess to demonstrate the kinetic nature of
neon, captured first place in the Ann Arbor film festival in
1981. The idea was to animate neon using the human
body as a vehicle. This was accomplished by using a
human skeleton of "light wands" wired in series and
sealed in plastic sheeves. These were held to a
jumpsuit-like garment via Velcro straps. Each suit was
custom-fitted to a dancer and joined together by a belt
worn around the waist. Two leather-insulated connections
in the back of the belt were the hook-up between the
suits and the transformers located off stage.

Designer: Richard Griendling
               Elizabethtown, Kentucky
Fabricator: Richard Griendling with the help of 15
               Hardin Country (Kentucky) high school
               students
Client: Coca-Cola Bottling of Elizabethtown,
               Kentucky

The work was the direct result of Richard Griendling's
one-year stint as artist in residence at the Bozeman,
Montana, school where his interest in photorealism and
surrealism turned to a fascination in the interplay of two-
and three-dimensional space. Funding for the project
came primarily by the Coca-Cola Bottling Co. of
Elizabethtown, Kentucky. The body cast process involved
placing plaster-impregnated gauze over the skin and
clothing of subjects, much like one would do for a
broken arm or leg; the insides of each cast figure were
reinforced with fiberglass which were adhered to the van
with resin. The sculptures were then sanded extensively
before receiving three coats of paint.

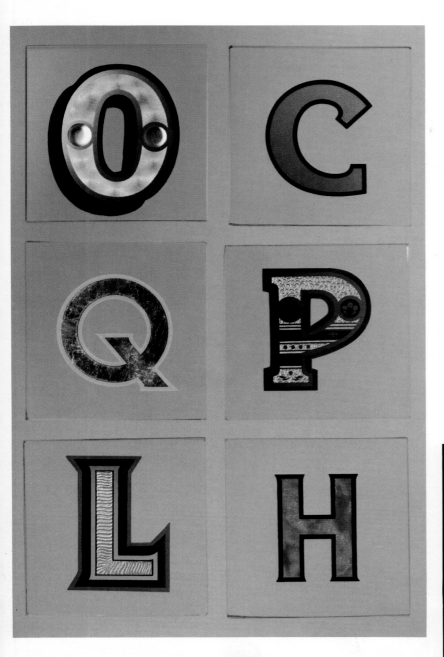

Designer: Bob Mitchell
Fabricator: Bob Mitchell
               Escondido, California
Client: Gold Leaf Sample Case

These are several examples from Bob Mitchell's sample case which show off some of the many possible gold leaf techniques that can be employed on any given sign. The "O," for example, is outlined in 23K gold with inset watch crystals, a lemon matte twist, Prussian blue, and green outline and a drop shadow. The "P" is outlined in 23K gold with white matte gold and lemon gold Damar varnish.

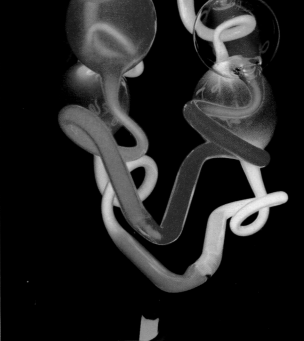

Designer: Jimmy Morris
Fabricator: Jimmy Neon
               Bremerton, Washington

A new generation of artists is experimenting with various forms of abstract neon. The juxtaposition of light, color, and shape all help create a new perception of what neon can do.

Designer: G & B Optics
Fabricator: G & B Optics
Client: Orion Film's tradeshow exhibit

The fiber optic animated sequence is created for Orion
Film's 6 × 12-ft. tradeshow exhibit. The lettering on the
display is 2 ft. tall.

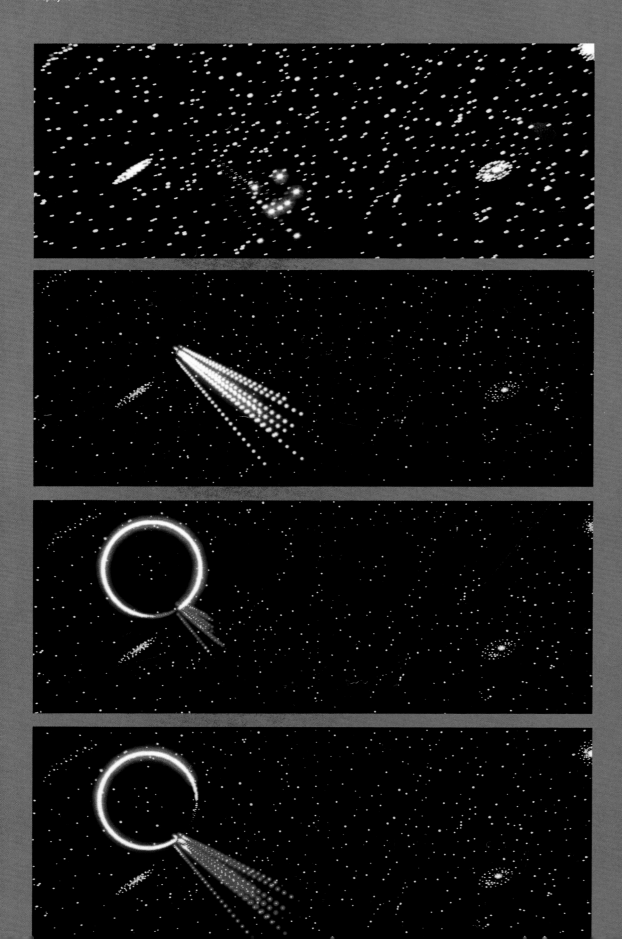

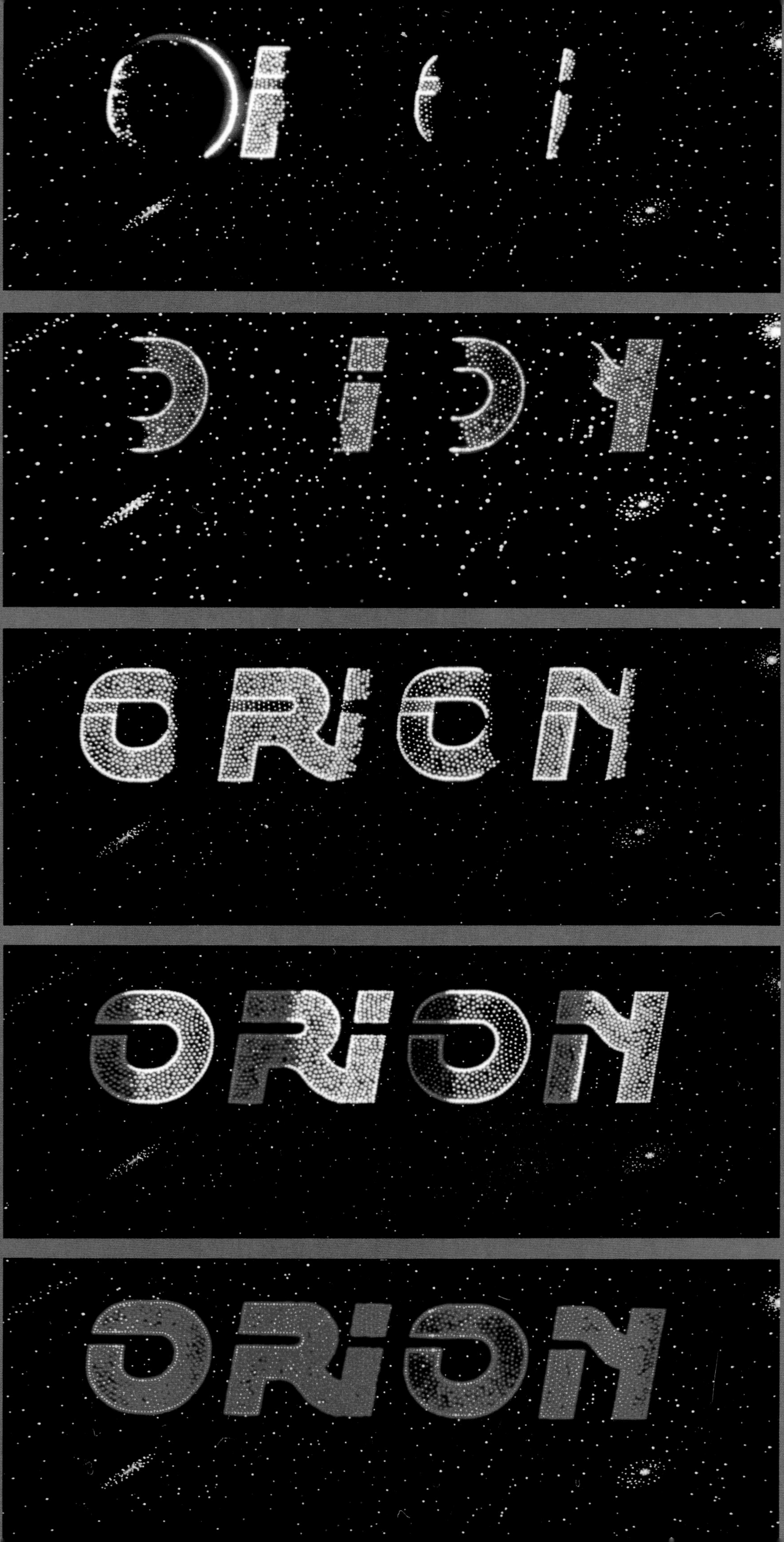
ORION
ORION
ORION

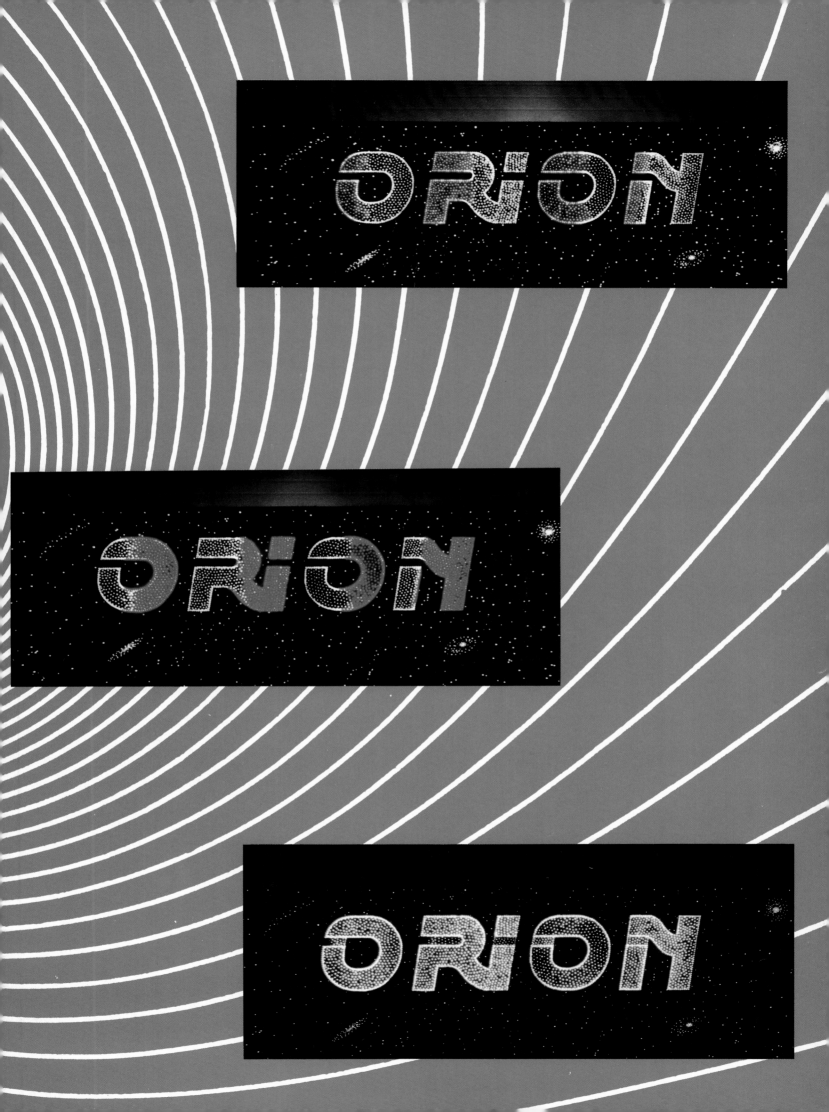

SIGN SIGN
SIGN SIGN
SIGN SIGN
SIGN SIGN
SIGN SIGN
SIGN SIGN
SIGN SIGN

8

Miscellaneous

The title of this chapter should clue the reader on what to expect—almost everything and anything. This chapter shows the diversity of what work sign companies and design firms are handling these days.

For example, Gary Volkman designed and fabricated the cover art for the October 1984 issue of *Signs of the Times*. By some standards, Volkman's 16 × 22 in. design is not a sign at all, but a sleek piece of advertising art. The truth is—it's both. As advertising, the piece has gone through the traditional graphic arts processes. It's been photographed, color separated, plated, and printed. As a sign, it was constructed using techniques germane to that industry: It's been gilded, marbled, hand painted, screen printed, sanded, and varnished. A technically proficient sign maker familiar with the ''lost art'' crafts, would be capable of fashioning this ''sign cover,'' but very few others in the related graphic arts field would have the expertise.

Indeed, this Miscellaneous chapter contains quite a few examples of the advertising's community reliance upon the sign trade. The most visible applications are the graphics and point-of-purchase displays. There are hundreds of companies in the trade which now deal exclusively in these burgeoning offshoot industries. What these firms manufacture are not so much on-premise identification as off-premise advertising. Similar to the outdoor advertising industry (another branch of the sign family tree) these companies often do not sell a product, as much as they provide a service.

Another new aspect of the sign business is the manner in which advertising agencies are using the industry. They see sign makers as innovative creators of exhibits and displays. This area is no longer the exclusive domain of the traditional exhibit and display builder. For example, Procter & Gamble contacted and contracted with City Lights Neon, in Cincinnati, Ohio, to help design and fabricate a complex display to help introduce its product "New Tide." This involved the custom fabrication of a "neon tunnel" which literally "focused" on a Tide logo in neon and backlit by lasers. This was reinforced with rear projected images of the new package design. To complete the exhibit required coordinating the efforts of vendors from many segments of many industries. On this project, the sign industry assumed a key role. And in the future it will play a much larger role in the scheme of things than ever before.

DESIGN
DESIGN
DESIGN
DESIGN
DESIGN

Designer: Cafe Calabash
                Calgary, Alberta, Canada
Photography: Klaus Berger
Client: Cafe Calabash

The neon outline around the top of the building can
reportedly be seen from many blocks away.

Designer: Everbrite Electric Signs, Inc.
Fabricator: Everbrite Electric Signs, Inc.
               South Milwaukee, Wisconsin
Client: Raleigh Bicycle Dealership

The sign was intended to gain product identity in dealers
where Raleigh is not the primary line.

Designer: Kit Hinrichs
               Johnson, Pedersen, Hinrichs & Shakery
               San Francisco, California
Fabricator: Triumph Advertising
               New York, New York
Client: Pennsylvania Station (Manhattan)

Billed as the "world's largest commercial transparency,"
this 10 × 102-ft. composite of photographic images of
New York City (taken from a helicopter) delivers its
message to over 5 million travelers who pass through
Penn Station each month. The project, conceived by
Livingston/Sirutis advertising agency, Belmont, California,
consists of 27 separate panels spliced together in an
airplane hanger. It took a five-man crew two days to
mount the image. Creative director was Jerry Leonhart
and copy director was Jack Reeves, both from
Livingston/Sirutis.

Designer: Nikon Advanced Products Co., Inc.
Fabricator: Nikon Advanced Products Co., Inc.
              Tokyo, Japan
Client: Takahishi Sports Store

This NAP board has a capacity to store 120 different
pictures and is used to promote manufacturers whose
products are sold in the store. It is floodlit from below at
night.

Designer: Rohm & Haas Company
Fabricator: Rohm & Haas Company
               Philadelphia, Pennsylvania
Client: Ski

Multi-surfaced graphics are employed on this prototype
sign designed by Rohm & Hass to display the
possibilities of the company's plastic face products.

Designer: Charles Barnard
Fabricator: Ad-Art, Inc.
               Stockton, California
Client: Hollywood Park

One of three identical monument displays at intersections
which border the track, the sign utilizes a single-line
readout. The reverse channel letters are finished in bronze
and backlit by neon. The fabricated metal background has
an architectural "stucco" finish.

Designer: Ferranti-Packard
Fabricator: Ferranti-Packard
               Mississauga, Ontario, Canada
Client: Montreal Olympic Stadium

Telespot III advertising signs were developed by the
designer. The total system for this client comprises six
signs (three large outdoor signs and three smaller indoor
signs) all in full matrix format.

Designer: American Sign & Indicator Corp./Div. of
               BRAE Corp.
Fabricator: American Sign & Indicator
               Spokane, Washington

A four-color scoreboard hangs over Reunion Arena, home
of the Dallas Mavericks.

Designer: Ferranti-Packard
Fabricator: Ferranti-Packard
                Mississauga, Ontario, Canada
Client: Hamilton Place

The computerized electronic advertising sign called
Telespot III was developed by the designer. This is
installed at Hamilton Place in Toronto.

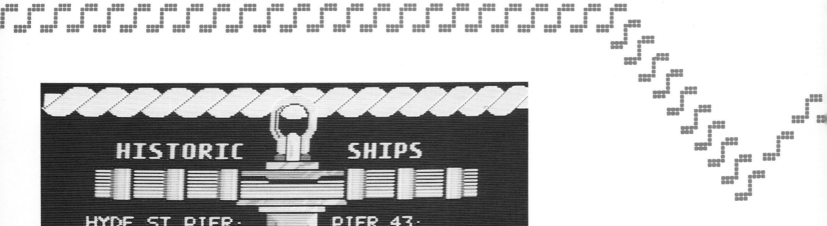

Designer: Bay Area Teleguide
              San Francisco, California
Fabricator: Chronicle Videotex, Inc.
              Toronto, Ontario, Canada
Client: San Francisco

Described as a computerized electronic guidebook, a videotex display provides comprehensive "pages" of words and graphics about shops, attractions, restaurants, services, sports, recreation, and events. Any number of the videotex displays can be located around the city.

Designer: Eclipse 3 Design, Ltd.
                 Winnipeg, Manitoba, Canada
Fabricator: Spectralite 70 Ltd.
Client: Pepsico
Floating 6 in. off the wall and mounted on
polycarbonate, the signs are backlit by orange
neon.

Designer: Signs by George
Fabricator: Signs by George
             North Mankato, Minnesota
Client: 7–UP

The sign was laid out by scaling a 7–Up can, using a sliderule. Painted bulletin enamel paints were used.

Designer: Eclipse 3 Design, Ltd.
             Winnipeg, Manitoba, Canada
Fabricator: Spectralite 70 Ltd.
Client: 7–UP

Floating 6 in. off the wall and mounted on polycarbonate, the signs are backlit by orange neon.

Designer: Everbrite Electric Signs, Inc.
Fabricator: Everbrite Electric Signs, Inc.
South Milwaukee, Wisconsin
Client: Lite Beer

The Revolving Edgelit Panels incorporate customer graphics. The frame is metalized to enhance overall image.

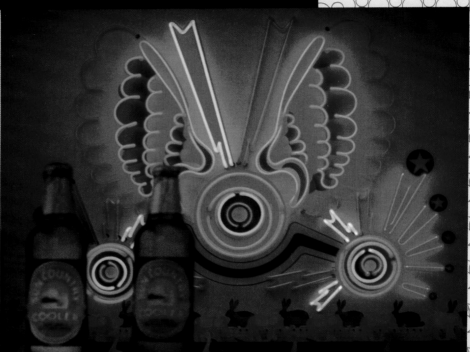

Designer: Say It In Neon, Inc.
Fabricator: Say It In Neon, Inc.
New York, New York
Client: Sun Country Cooler

For use in showrooms and tradeshows, the sign is constructed of neon and acrylic.

Designer: Anheuser Busch
Fabricator: Sign Art
Hawaiian Gardens, California
Client: Michelob

The pictorial work tor this handpainted truck was done by Don Wise of Sign Art.

Designer: Utilimaster Corp.
Wakarusa, Indiana
Fabricator: Everbrite Electric Signs, Inc.
South Milwaukee, Wisconsin
Client: Anheuser-Busch

Utilimaster Corp., a truck building firm that produces specialized truck bodies, now markets a line of "six packs" to interested soft drink and beer manufacturers. The trucks are used for short delivery runs to retail stores but their biggest use is for rental purposes at parties, fairs, etc. Many of the trucks come complete with spigots and chilled beer. The patent-pending cans are made of clear polycarbonate and are screen printed flat on the second surface by Everbrite Electric. Subsequently, they are cold bent by hand to fit custom-made frames on the trucks. Made in exact proportion to a beverage can, the cans are lit by 6-ft. fluorescent tubes in the center of each can.

Designer: R.P. Shaw
Gahanna, Ohio

Wall mural is an 8 × 12-ft. restaurant wall in keeping with the 1920's theme. The brick and the style give a nostalgic appeal.

Designer: Barth Bros.
Fabricator: Barth Bros.
New Orleans, Louisiana
Client: New Orleans Mardi Gras parade

The Barth Bros. of New Orleans designed and constructed these figures, the dragon and the representation of Moloch, the ancient Philistine god to whom children were sacrificed by burning. The floats appeared in the New Orleans Mardi Gras parade.

Signs have been used since ancient times to identify makers of goods and renderers of services. To an illiterate populace, easy-to-understand illustrations were of prime importance. The tradition continues to this day. These signs are from Austria and Germany.

Designer: Martha Williams
Fabricator: The Wood Shop
Boyne City, Michigan
Client: Charlevoix Boat Club

The hand carved single-sided Pine sign is $2\frac{1}{2}$-ft × $2\frac{1}{2}$-ft., stained and painted with gold leaf lettering.

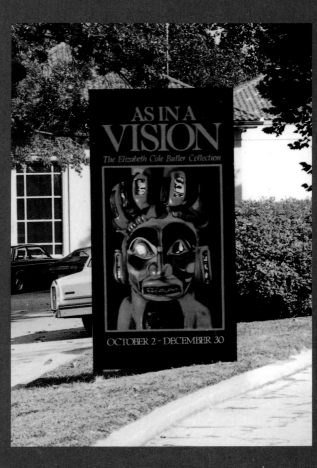

Designer: Carol Haralson
Fabricator: Western Sign Company
Tulsa, Oklahoma
Client: As in a Vision

The airbrushed pictorial of a color photo used for an Indian art exhibit is on 4 × 8-ft. plywood.

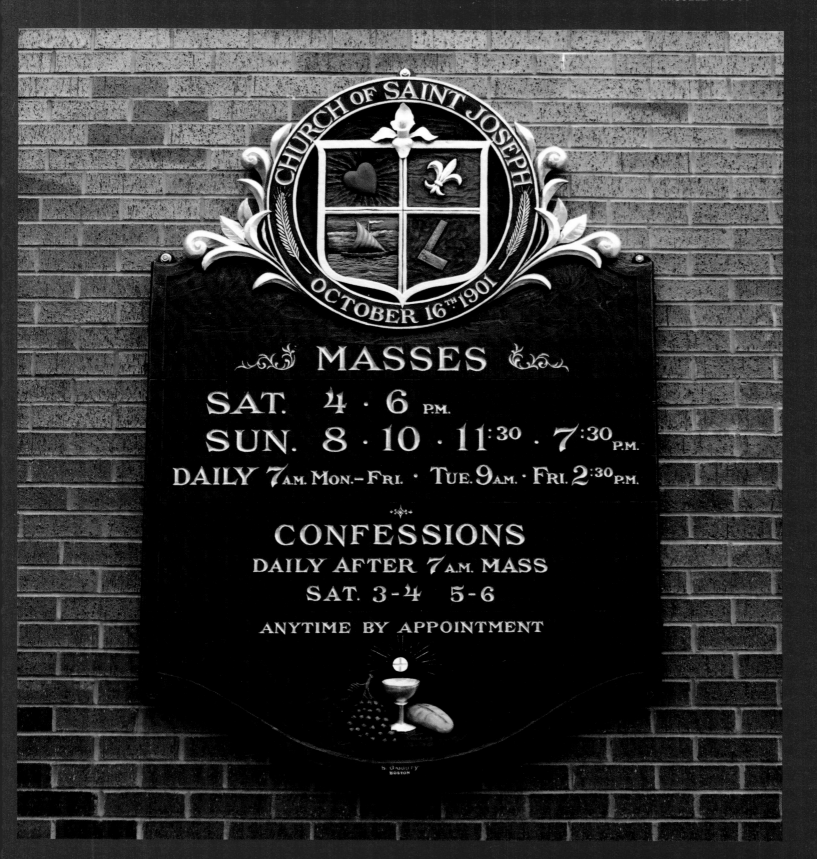

Designer: Susannah and Stephen Garrity
Fabricator: Garrity Carved Signs
                 Belmont, Massachusetts
Client: Church of Saint Joseph

The sign was hand carved from 2 1/8-in. thick
mahogany. Lettering and scrollwork are gilded 23K, with
symbols painted in long-lasting colors. The two middle
sections of the sign are easily removeable to affect
changes.

Designer: Computer Sign Systems Ltd.
Fabricator: Computer Sign Systems Ltd.
Markham, Ontario, Canada
Client: Canadian Pavilion of the 1982 World's
Fair

The computer-controlled neon sculpture/map was a focal point for the entry area to the Canadian Pavilion of the 1982 World's Fair in Knoxville, Tennessee. The map, which is a representation of Canada's major energy resources, consists of 77 vertical red neon tubes and shows the major energy resources with 54 smaller neon tubes powered by 64 high-voltage transformers and over 150 incandescent lamps. All of the neon tubes and incandescent lamps were computer-programmed in cycles with individual lengths varying from 20 seconds to 20 minutes. The display is now permanently installed in the lobby of the Department of External Affairs headquarters in Ottawa.

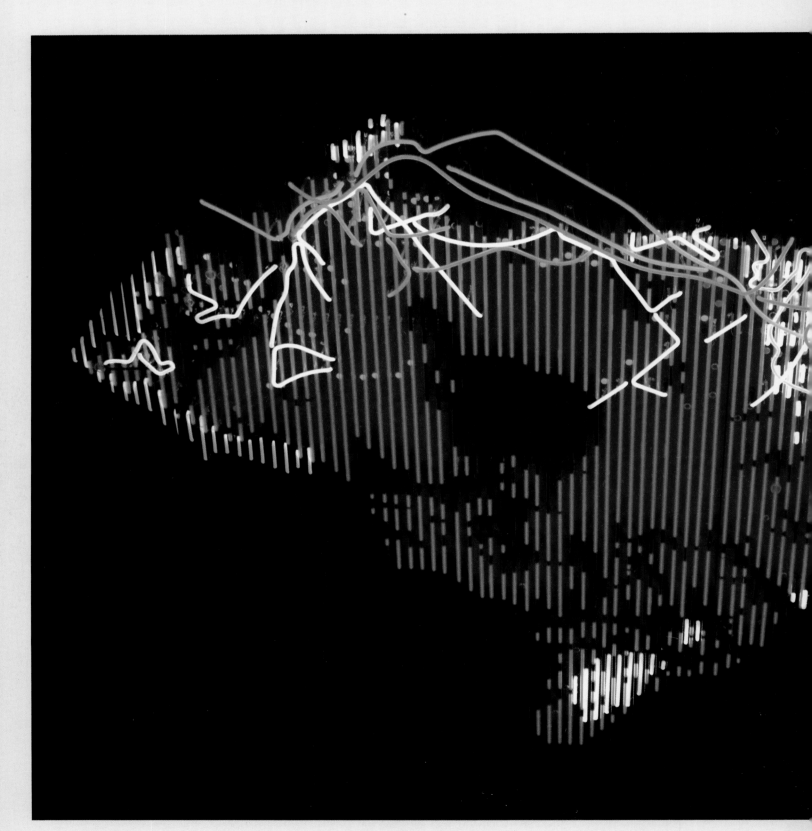

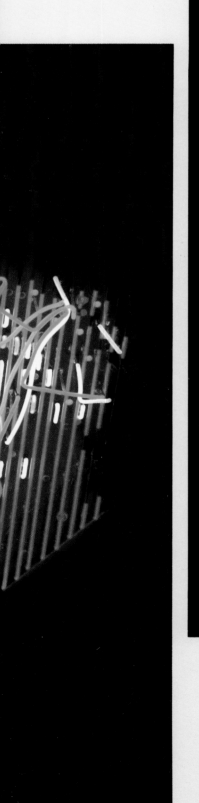

Designer: Gary Volkman
Fabricator: Gary Volkman
Denver, Colorado
Client: *Signs of the Times* magazine

Designed for a magazine cover, the 16 × 22-in. "sign" was entirely hand done except for the screen printed *Signs of the Times* logo. The masthead employs white gold; the lettering was done with water size and the border in quick size and spun, all of which was backed up with a clear overcoat and black japan. The "gold leaf" copy uses 23K burnished gold. The pictorial was taken from Alphonse Mucha. The side panels are marbled with turkey feathers and 3/4-in. bulletin fitches. The large pearl piece at the bottom was laid on Damar varnish.

Designer: Brian Marquis
              Great, Inc.
Fabricator: Light'n Up Neon
              Washington, D.C.
Client: Printing Industries of America

This neon sculpture was designed for a promotional poster printed and distributed at the 1985 National Printing Convention in Chicago.

Designers: Karen Heisler, Joanne Crawford
Fabricator: Neon Neon
              San Francisco, California
Client: Flying Service

The neon sign has been restored by Neon Neon to its former grandeur.

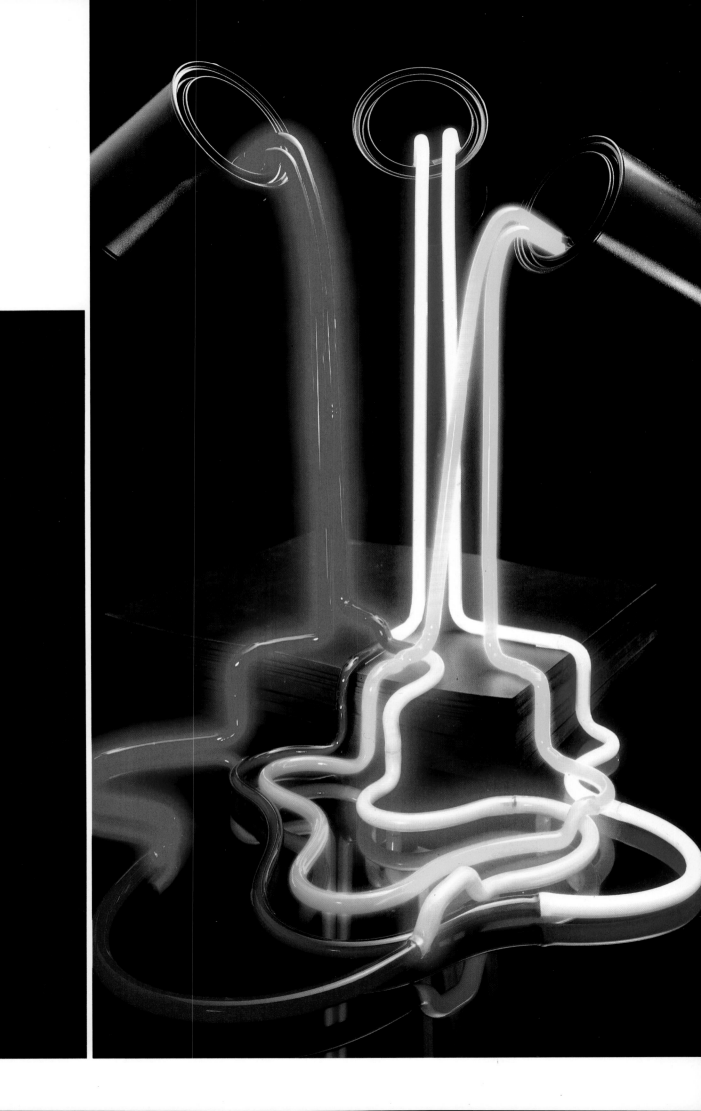

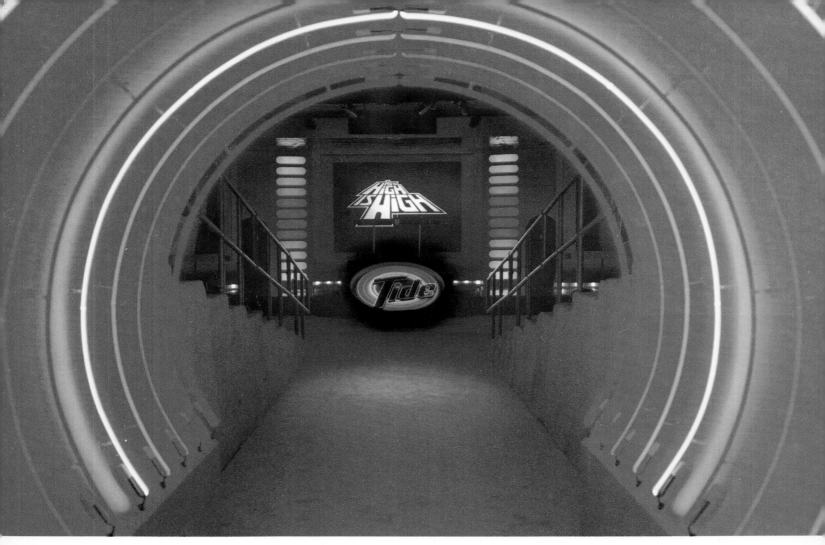

Fabricator: Adex
             Cincinnati, Ohio
Client: Procter + Gamble

City Lights Neon, Cincinnati, Ohio, designed three
different bands of neon, each of which flashes in chasing
sequence. The glass used is ruby red, clear gold and
neo-ruby.

Designer: City Lights Neon
Fabricator: City Lights Neon
                Cincinnati, Ohio
Client: Procter + Gamble

The Tide sign is constructed of 5-ft. diameter Baltic Birch board covered with white matte style Formica®. On the back of the sign is a sheetmetal pan box complete with lids and louvers. This houses the transformers, dimmers and electrodes. The front of the sign is constructed of custom sheetmetal letters sprayed in enamel and outlined by 12mm ultra-blue and clear gold glass. The sign is backlit by lasers set up by Imageering, Boston, Massachusetts. The Tide boxes in the back are rear projected screens.

DESIGNERS

A

Ad-Art, Inc., 72, 154
Ad Laser, 208
Admiral Signworks Corporation, 56
Ad Shoppe, 56
Albright, Larry, 198
Alcagi, Doug, 79
Allan Sign Man Corporation, 144
Allen, Robert H., Jr., 149
Allpoints Advertising, 64
American Sign & Indicator Corp., Div. of BRAE Corp., 228
Ancient Mariner, 48, 50
Anderson, Gary, 30, 33, 111
Andreson Typographics, 111
Anheuser Busch, 234
Artglo Sign Company, 70, 152
Art Group, Inc., 68
Artistic Signs, 105

B

Balsly, George, 52
Barham-Fancher, 168
Barlow, Frank, 77
Barnard, Charles, 227
Barth Bros., 236
Baty, Mark, 138
Bay Area Teleguide, 230
Bechtel Corporation, 154
Beer, Henry, 41
Bell Neon Sign Company, 185
Bemel, Susan, 27
Beverly Hills Motor Car Society, 163
Black, Gib, 100
Bohlman, Robin A., 88
Bonar, Ted, 61
Bond, Bob, 163
Brown, Koby & Levingston Advertising, 126
Byrd, Melissa, 123

C

Cafe Calabash, 224
Capon, John, 31
Carey, Ed, 120
Carpenter, Jerry, 141
Carrisa, Anthony, 28
Carter, Jim, 113
Cawthorn, Bill, 127
Chinook Plastics, 29, 37
Christman Studios, Inc., 43, 57, 141, 151, 173
City Lights Neon, 246
Claudea Neon Federal, 132
CMR Sign & Lighting, 134
Collender, Jim, 96
Colorado Woodsmith, Inc., 115, 186
Computer Sign Systems, Ltd., 242
Concannon, Bill, 58, 94, 198, 209
Concrete Monument, 139
Cooke, Jay, 31, 82, 155
Cook's Sign Company, 74
Costa, Robert, 98
Crawford, Charles M., 27, 121

Crawford, Joanne, 244
Creative Design, 98
Culbertson, Jim, 58
Culler, Pat, 71

D

Daly & Daly, 39
Daniels, Bruce A., 157
Davis, Virgil, 126
Deco Neon, 59
Design Group, The, 91
D. I. Design & Developmental Consultants, Inc., 185
Dillon, Daniel R., 128
Dobney, Jim, Art Service, 42
Doon, Bonny, Art Glass, 202, 204
Dr. Neon, 93, 97
Dungan, Starla, 174
DuVall, Sam, 94

E

Eclipse 3 Design, Ltd., 232, 233
Ehrlich-Rominger, Architects, 139
Everbrite Electric Signs, Inc., 225, 234
EverGreene Painting Studios, Inc., 210, 211, 213, 214

F

Fancher, Jim, 19
Fancher, Barham, Architects, Inc., 19
Faverman, Mark, 161
Fells, Henry, 40, 76, 116
Ferranti-Packard, 228, 229
Ferula, A. P., 162
Fine, Sarah, 83
Fiory & Wong, 96
Forbes, John, 202, 204
Frazier, John, 46
Fuller, Neal, 87
Fulton Advertising, 177

G

Galloway, James, 81
Gannett Outdoor of New Jersey, United Sign Division, 80
Gardner Signs, Inc., 88
Gariepy, Raymond, 83
Garnett, G., 63
Garrity, Stephen, 22, 32, 76, 241
Garrity, Susannah, 22, 32, 76, 241
G & B Optics, 218
Giordano, Kim, 151
GNU Group, 79
Goldman & Associates, 78
Graboski, Tom, Associates, 15, 171
Graphic Designs, 103
Graphics Hardware Company, 179, 181
Graphic Systems, 100, 104
Greater Pittsburgh Neon, 58
Green, Larry, 128

Griendling, Richard, 216
Griffin, Sharon, 91

H

Hamby, David, 172
Hannaman, Ed, 114
Hannukaine, John F., 47, 117, 124, 136
Hansen Lind Meyer, P.C., 165
Hanson, Craig, 168
Haralson, Carol, 240
Harding, David, 128, 163
Harris, Betsy, 191
Hayden, Tom, 210
Hayes, Gil, 30
Heath, W., & Company, 20
Heisler, Karen, 94, 244
Hinrichs, Kit, 225
Historic Design Associates, 28, 116
Holliday, Gail, 45, 195
Houston-Hobbs, Cia, 182
Hucall, M., 135
Hyde, Greg, 31

I

Idea Design, 63
Indreland, Glennis, 123
Inner City Neon, 90
Innervisons for Hair, 64
Ireland, Ross, 22, 101, 103
Irwin, Ralph, 53

J

Jack, N., 135
Jackson, Mike, 24, 44, 113, 173
Jacome, David E., 114
Jalbert, Normand, 15, 16
Janssen, Bruce, 149, 187
Jenks, David, 91
Johnson, Mike, 139
Johnson, Pedersen, Hinrichs & Shaker, 225

K

Kaiser Advertising, Inc., 129
Karlsberger & Associates, Inc., 156
Keene, Mike, 75
Keese, Larry, 179, 181
Keg'n Cleaver, 78
Kenne, Brooks, 171
Killian, Roland, 54
Kite, Donna, 158
Knecht, Keith, 110
Kuzma, Ben, 160

L

Lajeunesse, Michel, 22, 65, 182
Langhorst, H., 86

Larrivee, Wendy, 25
Lee, Alice, 140
Leonard, Dick, 186
Longacre, Janna, 205
Longanecker, Mike, 36
Loya, Rick, 82
Luffman, John, 195

M

Madsen, Don, 128
Mando, Frank, 80
Maple, Jeff, 39
Markle, Robert, 92
Marquis, Brian, 245
Marshall, D. & J., 148
McKitchens, Larry, 175
McFaddin, Roy, 119
McMillan, Del, Design Group, Ltd., 74
Media 5, 35
Media Concepts Corporation, 21
Minidis, J., 135
Mitchell, Bob, 217
Monigle, Glenn, & Associates, Inc., 106
Moretta & Sheehy, Architects, 140
Morris, Bob, 122
Morris, Jimmy, 217
Mysse, Steve, 184

N

Namour, Reg, 117
Neon Products Ltd., 17, 102, 124, 132, 143
Nikon Advanced Products Co., Inc., 226
Nilsson, Lillian, 142

O

Oatis, Mark, 46, 47
Oestreicher, T., 201
Ollinger, Bill, 193
On Board Signs, 86
Oxford, Curt, Woodcarver, 18, 19

P

Pampu, Cary W., 132
Parker Sign Company, Inc., 187
Partners, The, 153
Pasquarell, Michael, Association, 136
Pawley, Perry, 194
Pedley, Francis, 107
Perkins and Will, 157
Pioneer Signs, 128
Piskule, Raymond O., 170
Pohl, Eric E., 206
Poitras, Maurice, 83
Port Authority of New York and New Jersey, 183
Pritchard, James, 24
Pritchard, Lesley, 75
Prosch, Heinz, & Associates Designs, Inc., 126

Q

Quinn, Jerry O., 171

R

Rankin, Laura, 162
Reaves, Tom, 122
Reed Design Associates, 174
Robbins, Glenn, 176
Rodgers, Ron, 107
Rohm & Haas Company, 227
Rohrs, Carl, 44, 122
Romanoff, U., & Associates, 150
Rouse, Charles, 168
Rudolph, Andra, 44
Ruge, Raymond A., 116
Runquist, Richard, 84
Russo, Eckert Morton, 119
Ryan, G., Design, Inc., 169, 188
Ryan, Gerard, 150
Ryan, James P., Associates, Architects, 14, 38, 43

S

Saarl, Peter, 215
Sack, Dan, 162
Satterfield Art Products, 45
Say It in Neon, Inc., 38, 234
Schiess, Christian, 200, 201, 205, 216
Schnute, Ronda, 82
Schnute, William, 41, 82
Shaw, R. P., 235
Sheehan, Mike, 18
Sign Cellar, The, 42
Signmaker, The, 32
Signs by Ben, 28
Signs by George, 233
Signs by Liza, 119
Signs Systems, Inc., 89
Sign Wizards, 101
Sikorski, Tony, Studio, 99
Simco Sign, 85
Simmons, Doug, 26
Slater Associates, 195
Smallwood, Mike, 191
Smathers, Roger K., 105, 125, 145
Smith, Ken, 54, 56
Snow, Sherry, 41, 137
Soltendieck, Christien, 57
Sonderman, Joe, Inc., 159, 170, 190, 192
Sorgman, Ken, 33, 115
State Sign Corporation, 133
Stevens, Mike, 95
Stolz Advertising, 45

Storek + Storek, 60
Strategic Identities, Inc., 138
Suba, Bruce, 202, 204
Suba Neon, 202, 204

T

Tampa Outdoor Graphics, Inc., 190
Tanaka, John, 62
Tarnoff Graphics, 87
Taylor Group, 172
Trammel Crow Company, 128

U

Unica Design, Inc., 36
United Signs, Inc., 92
Utilimaster Corp., 235

V

Van Laan & Associates, 171
Van Ryan, G., Design, Inc., 174
Van Swearingen, Kirk, 84, 86
Vigliotti, Tony, 168
Volkman, Gary, 243
Vomela Corp., 201

W

Ward, Dan, 145
Watt, Don, & Associates, 52, 144
West, Robin, Design, 120
White, Carol, 121
White Lettering & Art, 70
White, Paul, 17
Williams, Douglas, 35, 100
Williams, Martha, 240
Withuhn, Charles, 46
Wittke, Jim, 133
Wood, Cohen, Leonard & Busch, 186
Woodsmith, Donald E., 29, 77, 104

Y

Young Electric Sign Company, 73

Z

Zachlem, Michelle, 142

FABRICATORS

A

Aargon Neon, 58, 209
Acralume Signs & Displays Ltd., 52, 144
Action Sign Company, 172
Ad-Art, Inc., 72, 154, 227
Adex, 247
Ad Laser, 208
Admiral Signworks Corporation, 56
Albright, Larry, 198
Allan Sign Man Corporation, 144
Allpoints Advertising, 64
American School of Neon, 184
American Sign & Indicator Corp., 228
Ancient Mariner, 48, 50, 54, 56, 57
Andco Industries Corporation, 149
April Day Studio, Inc., 45, 195
Architectural Signage and Display, 129
Architecture Group, The, 117
Arrow Sign Company, 54, 79, 140
Art Forum, Inc., 53
Artglo Sign Company, Inc., 69, 152
Artistic Signs, 105

B

Barth Bros., 236
Baty Art + Sign, Inc., 138
Bell, Don, & Company, 174
Bell Neon Sign Company, 185
Bemel Carved Sign, 27
Blanchett Neon Ltd., 132
Bloomington Sign, 30, 33, 111
Bonar, Ted, 61
Bond, Bob, 163
Boulder Sign Studio, 41

C

California Rehabilitation Center, 163
Carey & Fort Woodcarvers, 120
Cavanaugh Art & Design, 19, 168
Central Advertising, 14
Central Rede Sign Company, 162
Cherry Lane Studios, 150
Chinook Plastics, 29, 37
Christman Studios, 43, 57, 141, 151, 173
Chronicle Videotex, Inc., 230
City Lights Neon, 246
Classic Sign and Mirror, 18
Classic Signs & Designs, 142
Claude Neon Federal, 132
CMR Sign & Lighting, 134
Colorado Woodsmiths, 115, 142, 172, 186
COMCO Architectural & Electrical Signing, 41, 137
Comet Neon & Plastic Signs, 127
Computer Sign Systems Ltd., 242
Concannon, Bill, Sculptor, 94, 198
Cooke's, Jay, Sign Shop, 31, 82, 155
Cook's Sign Company, 74
Corbin, Paul, 106
Creation Vieil Art, 22, 65, 182
Creator's Touch, Inc., 151

Crystal Graphics, Inc., 186
Cypress Carving Ltd., 22, 25, 78, 101, 103

D

Deco Neon, 59
Dillon, Daniel R., Design Associates, 128
Doughty, Ellis, 106
Dresden Graphics Sign Company, 52
Dr. Neon, 93, 97
Dwinnell's Central Neon Company, 88

E

Eastern Signs, 162
Eller-United Outdoor Sign Company, 39
Les Enseignes du Haut-Richelieu, 15, 16
Enseignes Poitras, Inc., 83
Environmental Graphic Arts, 64
Environmental Graphics, 194
ETM Graphics, 165
Everbrite Electric Signs, Inc., 225, 234, 235
EverGreene Painting Studios, Inc., 210, 211, 213, 214, 215

F

Ferranti-Packard, 228, 229
Fibremart Designs, Inc., 182
Fine Gold Lettering, 111
First Impression Sign Company, 84
First Neon Sign and Service Company, 160
Flying Colors, Inc., 161
Format Signs, 170
Freedom Signs, 191
Friedman Marble & Slate, 68

G

Galloway Signs, 81
Gannett Outdoor of New Jersey, 80
Gardner Signs, Inc., 88
Garrity Carved Signs Company, 22, 32, 76, 241
G & B Optics, 218
GDC Sign Studio, 175
Glover, Bob, Inc., 43
Graphic Designs, 26, 103
Graphicon Solutions, 80
Graphic Systems, Inc., 15
Graphic Systems International, Inc., 159
Grapiconcepts, 77
Greater Pittsburgh Neon, 58, 98
Griendling, Richard, 216

H

Habitat, Inc., 176
Hannaman, Ed, Sign Crafters, 114
Hannukaine, John F., Company, 47, 85, 117, 124, 136
Hayes, G. R., Signs, 30

Heath & Company, 42
Heath, W., & Company, 20, 141
Hico Resources, Inc., 148
Hoarel Sign Company, 36
Hollinger, Stevens, 95

I

Industrial Illustrations, 135
Inner City Neon, 38
Ireland, Ross, 78

J

Jackson Signs, 24, 44, 78, 113, 173
Jacome & Company, 114
Jimmy Neon, 217
Jirka, Brad, Designers, 184
J&K Sign Company, 99

K

Karlsberger & Associates, Inc., 156

L

Lajeunesse, Michel, 113
Light Images, Inc., 98
Light'n Up Neon, 244
Lite Craft Neon, Inc., 96
Local Neon Company, Inc., 94
Louviere, Scott, Sign Company, 126
Luttman, John, Woodcarver, 195

M

Macrographics, 136
Marschesci, Cork, 184
Mathis Company, The, 36
Matthews International Corp., 70
Maw and Company, Ltd., 153
McCarthy's, Paul, Carving Place, 21
McFaddin, Roy, Inc., 119
Melweb Signs, Inc., 171, 177
Mississippi Electric Signs, Inc., 123
Mitchell, Bob, 217

N

Neon, Neon, 60, 61, 94, 95, 96, 201, 244
Neon Products Ltd., 17, 102, 124, 132, 143
Neon Projects, 61
Nikon Advanced Products Co., Inc., 226
Nordquist Sign Company, 184
North Shore Sign Company, 123
Nu Art Signmaker, 87

O

Oak Leaves Studio, 41, 82

Olson Signs & Displays, 113
On Board Signs, 86
Other Sign Company, 68
Oxford, Curt, Woodcarver, 18, 19

P

Parker Sign Company, Inc., 187
Pedley, Francis, 107
Pioneer Signs, 128
Pritchard Carved Signs, 24

Q

Quality Signs & Designs, 25

R

Reed Design Associates, 174
Rodgers & Wiley, 107
Rohm & Haas Company, 227
Rohrs, Carl, 44
Rouse Sign & Graphics, 168
Routed Signs, Inc., 190
Rustic Designs, 74
Rustic Graphics, 158
Ryan, G., Design, Inc., 150, 169, 188
Ryan, James P., Associates, Architects & Planners, 90

S

Satterfield Art Productions, 45
Sawdust Creations, 83
Say It in Neon, Inc., 38, 234
Schiess, Christian, 200, 201, 205, 216
Sculptured Neon Company, 63
Shelley Signs, 150
Signage Systems Company, 122
Sign and Design, 184
Sign Art, 234
Sign Arts, 28, 116
Sign Classics, Inc., 139
Sign Force, 145
Signmaker, The, 32
Sign of Excellence, A, 163
Signs & Graphic Design, 46
Signs and Things, 27, 110, 121
Signs by Ben, 28
Signs by George, 233
Signs by Ken, 33, 115
Signs by Liza, 119
Signs by Mike, 75
Sign Shop, The, 39
Signs of Yesteryear, 191
Signs, Rohrs, 122
Signs South, 105, 125, 145
Sign Studio, The, 46, 47
Sign Systems, Inc., 89
Signtific Signs, 100, 104
Sign Wizards, 101
SmithCraft Manufacturing Company, 179, 181
Sonderman, Joe, Inc., 170

Southcoast Designs, 87
Spectralite 70 Ltd., 232, 233
State Sign Corporation, 133
Steamboat Woodsmith, 29, 77, 104
Suba Neon, 202, 204
Swanson, Jerry, 106
Sziba & Smolover Glass Carvers, 68

T

Talley Neon & Advertising, 138, 192
Tampa Outdoor Graphics, Inc., 190
Tanaka, John, 62
Ten Mile River Sign Company, 84, 86
Tishman Construction of Arizona, 157
Torrone, Frank, & Sons, Inc., 183
Triumph Advertising, 225
True Blue Design and Fabrication, 31

U

United Signs, Inc., 92
Upham, Joseph P., 205

V

Valley City Sign Company, 133

Van Ryan, G., Design, Inc., 174
Volkman, Gary, 243
Vomela Corp., 201

W

Washington, University of, Sign Shop, 91
West, Robin, Design, 120
Western Sign Company, 240
Whalen, Bob, 28, 116
White Lettering & Art, 70
White, Paul J., Woodcarver, 17, 121
Williams, Douglas, Woodcarving, 35, 100
Woodcarver Designs, Inc., 193
Woodfox Designs, 40, 76, 116
Wood Shop, The, 75, 148, 149, 187, 240

Y

Yerexneon, Inc., 63, 92, 206
Young Electric Sign Company, 73

Z

Zanetti, Al, Sign Studios, 119

CLIENTS

A

Aberdeen Federal Savings & Loan Association, 124
Academy of Russia Classical Ballet, 111
Alcoa South Carolina, Inc., 142
Aloe Vera of America, Inc., 141
American National Bank of Libertyville, 123
Anatole Hotel, 71
Andresen Typographics, 111
Anheuser-Busch, 235
Ankey's, 98
Apartment Lounge & Grill, 74
Arboretum, 149
Art Glass by England, 44
Arts Center, 148-149
As in a Vision, 240
Atelier Office Condominiums, 168
Aurora Borealis, 61
Avanti Trattoria, 87

B

Bankers Trust Harborside Building, New Jersey, 210
Bank of Beaufort, 122
Bank of Jackson, 123
Bay West Commerce Park, 190
Bellflower, 33
Bette's Ocean View Diner, 95
Beverly Hills Motor Car Society, 163
Billy's Bar & Grill, 85
Bi-plane sculpture, 206
Bloomington Winery, 30
Bob Overby Neonist, 114
Bodacious, 44
Bonny Doon Art Glass, 202, 204
Brandy's, 102
Broadway Dental Center, 117
Bryant Gardens, 195
Buffalo Gals Restaurant, 84

C

Cabrillo Bathhouse and East Beach Grill, 191
Cafe Calabash, 224
Camino de Vista, 168
Canadian Pavilion of the 1982 World's Fair, 242
Canal Street, 84
Cantina, 104
Cape Fear Memorial Hospital, 149
Capital Northwest Management Corporation, 136
Captain's Table, 100
Card Street, 27
Carr, Oliver T., Company, The, 212-213
Cedar Wood Plaza, 17
Charlevoix Boat Club, 240
Les Charron, 182
Chico Bicycle, 46
City Flair, 42-43
Claim Jumper Gift Shop, 24
Cleveland Playhouse Square Center, 160
Club Car, 75
Coca-Cola Bottling of Elizabethtown, Kentucky, 216
Colorado Woodsmiths, 115

Columbus Foundation, 152
Columbus Museum of Art, 152
Consolidated Fastrate Transportation Group, 132
Continental Bank, 144
Contour Blind & Shade, 54
Courtney South Beach, 182
Cove, The, 77
Creative Advantage, Inc., 113
Creekside at the Homestead, 184
Crown Building, 215
Crown Glass Studio, 47
Culbertson, Jim, 58
Cypress Semiconductor, 139

D

Dallux, 63
Davidson, Sam, 120
Deer Field, 173
Doc Holliday's Game Emporium, 92
Doll House, 21
Dresbach Hunt-Boyer Mansion, 120
Duds Shop, The, 32

E

Eadeh Rug Company, 40
Eagle Computer, 145
Eckert Morton Musso, 119
Economy Data Products, 138
Egyptian Theatre, 54-55
Elk River, 172
Elmwood Place, 162
ENB, 127
Estancia Primera, 142
Eureka Florist, 64
Evans Group, The, 129
Expresso Yourself, 94

F

Faces, 63
Fairwind Yacht Charters, 121
Ferdinand's Restaurant, 76
Fiorucci's, 58
Firehouse Bar-B-Que, 70
Five Station Offices, 174
Flying Service, 244
Foothills Hospital, 148
1421, 46
Futon to Sleep On, 56

G

Gazebo, The, 18
George III, 74
Glass Farmhouse, 210
Golden Gate Theatre, 95
Gold Leaf Sample Case, 217
Goudelock, 145
Green Parrot Restaurant & Bar, 93
Greenville National Bank, 125

H

Hamilton Place, 229
Hanger, The, 41
Hannaman, Ed, Sign Crafters, 114
Harloff Chevrolet, 41
Headlines, 96
Head to Toe, 26
Health One, 156-157
Healthwood, 169
Helane & Judy Beauty Salon, 28
Heritage Oaks, 191
Hilton, 89
Hoffman House, 76
Hollywood Park, 227
Home Builders Supply, 53
Hub, 36-37
Huntington Subdivision, 186
Hyde Park Walk, 195
Hy's Encore, 102

I

Innervisions for Hair, 64
Inn the Woods, 75
Iowa, University of, Hospital, 164-165
Iron Horse Resort, 186
Irwin & Company, 116
Izzy's, 81

J

Jackson Signs, 113
Jácome & Company, 114
Jim Culbertson, 58

K

Kathy's Pub, 101
Keg Lobster House, 103
Keg'n Cleaver, 78
King Khalid International Airport, Saudi Arabia, 154

L

Lafayette House, 151
Lake Cafe, 88-89
Lakehouse Condominiums, 187
Lakeside Office Estates, 173
Lakeview Mall, 14
Lane Bryant, 62
Larrivee Guitars, 25
Last Spike, 106-107
Latigo, 25
Laurel Street Station, 88
Lighthouse, The, 87
Lil' Ray's Po Boys, 105
Limited Company, The, 214
Lincoln Centre, 178-181
Lite Beer, 234

Lockheed Plan # 10, 134-135
Lodge, The, 78
London Wall Walk, 153
Lucy's Marina Fun Center, 39
Lumens, 216

M

Maggie's, 28
Mahfuz & Sons Rug Gallery, 24
Maison Milot, 83
Mallard Cove, 172
Market Lane, 31
Markleangeleo's Restaurant, 92-93
Marshall Estates, 174-175
Martín-Serényo, 57
McDonald's, 82
McFaddin, Roy, 118-119
Métamorphose Haute Coiffure, 16
Miami Lakes Athletic Club, 15
Micarelli Warner Art Studio, 112-113
Michaels Groups, The, 128
Michelob, 234
Miller, Howard, Clock Company, 133
Millpond Park Developers, 190
Missouri Historical Society, 151
Mole Hole, The, 26
Montreal Olympic Stadium, 228
Mony, 133
Mother Hyde's Kitchen, 101
MPSI Centre, 132
M.R. Ducks Restaurant & Oyster Bar, 105
Mr. Music, 36
MSA, 139
Music Box, 21
My Child's Destiny, 60

N

Nabozny Press Printing, 116
National Bank of Commerce, 126
National Register of Historic Places, 150
Navarre Cafe, 85
New Orleans Mardi Gras parade, 236-237
New York Bagel Factory, The, 33
New York Deli, The, 99
Niles Hotel and Bar, 107
North Carolina Zoological Park, 159
Nova: An Alberta Corporation, 143
#4-Fire/Water series, 205

O

Oasis Casino, 72
Ocean Walk Villas, 194
Office at Bay Point, 171
Office Complex, 170
Okefenokee Swamp Park, 158
Olin, 141
One from the Heart, 198
One Reading Center, 184
Orion Film's tradeshow exhibit, 218-219

P

Paddlewheel Casino in Las Vegas, 73, 211
Panache Sportswear, 29
Panowicz Jewelers, 47
Paradise Cafe, 94
Park Center, 171
Pastabilities, 80
Le Pédalier, 15
Peerless Wallpaper, 98
Pennsylvania Station (Manhattan), 225
Pepsico, 232
Pergament, 144
Pharmacist, 32
Philadelphia Sandwich Co., The, 80
Pickering Museum, 150
Picnic, 90
Pink Blue Flasher, 209
Pink Light Rope, 201
Platters Cafe 1955, 97
Playboy Club, 198
Pointe Resort, The, 175
Polse, Richard, 122
Portage Bay Galley, 91
Poster Gallery, The, 163
Potted Geranium, The, 17
Printing Industries of America, 244-245
Private Residence, 187
Procter & Gamble, 246-247

R

Raleigh Cycle Company of America, 225
Ramada Inn, 79
Rank Xerox, 136
Regency Center, 19
Rex Lumber, 22
Ridge Court Condominiums, 170
Risha, 41
Ritz Cafe, 94
River House Seafood, 77
Riverplace, 184-185
Ross Music, 43
Royal Bank, 124

S

Saint Joseph, Church of, 241
San Francisco, 230-231
Save on Foods, 48-51
Schnucks, 45
Scoops, 59
7-UP, 233
Sheraton Tucson El Conquistador, 100, 104
Sherwood Forest, 193
Shop 27, 65
Signs & Things, 110
Signs by Ken, 115
Signs by Liza, 119
Signs of the Times magazine, 243
Silversands, 174
Ski, 227
Smuggler's Cafe, 86
Snoopy's Ice Cream & Cookies, 60-61
Sound Emporium, 42
Southwood Corporation, 117

Spectrum Office Building, 177
Squire's East, 86
Steele's Jewellers, Ltd, 29, 37
Stowe Restoration, 31
Stowe School, 155
Straight Lines, 38
Strathcona Refinery, 132
Sugar Knoll, 195
Sun Country Cooler, 234
Sun Spot, The, 19
Sweet Caroline's, 103
Systech, 137

T

Takahishi Sports Store 226
Tallulah's Hair Design, 18
Tamarack Restaurant & Lounge, 70
Temptations, 57
Teradyne, 140
Terrace Food Shops, 39
Theatre Mural, 106
Things from the Sea Scrimshaw, 27
Told!, 205
Trumps, 68
Tucson Medical Center, 157
Twigs, 22

V

Very Virginia Beach, 56
Vérité Mensonge, 83
Victoria Ward Ltd., 35
Le Vieil Art, 23
Violets & Victorian Lace, 30
Virginia M. McCune Community Arts Center, 148-149

W

Wardrobe Service, 52
Water Works Home, 176
West End Health Club, 43
Western Energy Inc., 134
Westland Center Shopping Mall Emporium, 38
Wet 'n' Wild, 20
Whiskey Creek, 83
Wianno Place, 121
Wilmot Creek, 188-189
Wilson's Harborplace Flower Market, 45
Woodlake, 192
World Trade Center, 183

X

Xerox Corporation, 128

Y

Yorkshire Trust, 126

Z

Zach's, 96